Introducing ArcGIS API 4 for JavaScript

Turn Awesome Maps into Awesome Apps

Rene Rubalcava

Apress®

Introducing ArcGIS API 4 for JavaScript

Rene Rubalcava
Rialto, California, USA

ISBN-13 (pbk): 978-1-4842-3281-1   ISBN-13 (electronic): 978-1-4842-3282-8
https://doi.org/10.1007/978-1-4842-3282-8

Library of Congress Control Number: 2017960885

Cover image designed by Freepik

Managing Director: Welmoed Spahr
Editorial Director: Todd Green
Acquisitions Editor: Louise Corrigan
Development Editor: James Markham
Technical Reviewer: Massimo Nardone
Coordinating Editor: Nancy Chen
Copy Editor: Kim Wimpsett
Compositor: SPi Global
Indexer: SPi Global
Artist: SPi Global

Distributed to the book trade worldwide by Springer Science+Business Media New York, 233 Spring Street, 6th Floor, New York, NY 10013. Phone 1-800-SPRINGER, fax (201) 348-4505, e-mail orders-ny@springer-sbm.com, or visit www.springeronline.com. Apress Media, LLC is a California LLC and the sole member (owner) is Springer Science + Business Media Finance Inc (SSBM Finance Inc). SSBM Finance Inc is a **Delaware** corporation.

For information on translations, please e-mail rights@apress.com, or visit www.apress.com/rights-permissions.

Apress titles may be purchased in bulk for academic, corporate, or promotional use. eBook versions and licenses are also available for most titles. For more information, reference our Print and eBook Bulk Sales web page at www.apress.com/bulk-sales.

Any source code or other supplementary material referenced by the author in this book is available to readers on GitHub via the book's product page, located at www.apress.com/9781484232811. For more detailed information, please visit www.apress.com/source-code.

Printed on acid-free paper

Table of Contents

About the Author

Rene Rubalcava has been working in the field of GIS for about 15 years now and has been developing custom applications for most of that time. He managed custom GIS development for the LA County Sanitation Districts, has done some consulting and freelancing over the years, and has been working for Esri since 2015. He works on the ArcGIS API for JavaScript and other projects. He maintains a blog, odoe.net, on spatial development, particularly focused on the ArcGIS API for JavaScript, and he runs an active YouTube channel (`https://www.youtube.com/c/renerubalcava`). He also wrote a book on the previous version of the API, called *ArcGIS Web Development* (Manning, 2014).

About the Technical Reviewer

Massimo Nardone has more than 23 years of experience in security, web/mobile development, cloud computing, and IT architecture. His true IT passions are security and Android.

He currently works as the chief information security officer (CISO) for Cargotec Oyj and is a member of the ISACA Finland Chapter board. Over his long career, he has held many positions including project manager, software engineer, research engineer, chief security architect, information security manager, PCI/SCADA auditor, and senior lead IT security/cloud/SCADA architect. In addition, he has been a visiting lecturer and supervisor for exercises at the Networking Laboratory of the Helsinki University of Technology (Aalto University).

Massimo has a master of science degree in computing science from the University of Salerno in Italy, and he holds four international patents (related to PKI, SIP, SAML, and proxies). Besides working on this book, Massimo has reviewed more than 40 IT books for different publishing companies and is the coauthor of *Pro Android Games* (Apress, 2015).

CHAPTER 1

Introduction

The ArcGIS API for JavaScript has evolved over the years to include new features that can take advantage of updates in ArcGIS Server and ArcGIS Online. The move to version 4 of the API is one of the biggest leaps in technology and features since its initial release. This version of the API introduces some new concepts for developers and makes 3D scenes easier for developers to add to their applications.

Where to Get the ArcGIS API

You can find more information about the API at https://developers.arcgis.com/javascript/latest.

Key Concepts

The ArcGIS API 4 for JavaScript embraces some concepts included in earlier versions of the API and introduces some new concepts. These are discussed in more detail through the book but are detailed briefly here:

- *Asynchronous Module Definition (AMD)*: This is the module system used by Dojo and is well suited for larger application development.

© Rene Rubalcava 2017
R. Rubalcava, *Introducing ArcGIS API 4 for JavaScript*,
https://doi.org/10.1007/978-1-4842-3282-8_1

- *Maps, layers, and views*: The map, with its layers and view relationship, is key. A map is a data source that can be linked to multiple views.

- *Accessors*: Accessors are powerful implementations of the API that provide a rich suite of features.

- *Collections*: These are array-like data stores that can also emit change events.

- *Promises*: The API has always used promises for asynchronous operations, but they play an even more important role in version 4.

- *Widgets and the UI*: The widgets and UI of the Map in the API have been completely rewritten and rearchitected for version 4.

- *Web scenes and local scenes*: Scenes are an exciting addition to the JavaScript API because they bring 3D capabilities into the hands of developers.

Things You Need to Know

I think it's fair to say that you should have some basic programming experience if you are reading this book. If you have JavaScript experience, that would be even better because this book will not cover JavaScript basics. There are plenty of resources you can find online to get caught up with JavaScript, and I recommend you do.

You don't need to know geographic information systems (GISs). I'm working under the assumption you know what a map is, and that's all.

AMD

For the purposes of this book, you won't need to worry too much about the AMD used in the ArcGIS API for JavaScript. All the samples in this book will be using ES2015,[1] and you can compile them to AMD with Babel[2] and GruntJS.[3]

What you do need to know is that the code you write for your ArcGIS JavaScript API applications will need to compile to AMD to use the Dojo loader[4].

Let's get started!

---

[1]https://babeljs.io/docs/learn-es2015/
[2]https://babeljs.io/
[3]http://gruntjs.com/
[4]http://dojotoolkit.org/reference-guide/1.10/loader/amd.
 html#loader-amd

3

CHAPTER 2

Getting Started

Let's stop fooling around and write some code. The following is the simple HTML page for your first application. All of the index.html pages in this sample will work off this one. You'll just be updating the JavaScript code as you go along.

```
1    <!DOCTYPE html>
2    <html>
3      <head>
4        <meta http-equiv="Content-Type" content="text/html;
         charset=utf-8">
5        <meta name="viewport" content="initial-scale=1,
         maximum-scale=1,user-scalable=no"/>\
6        <title>ArcGIS API for JavaScript 4</title>
7        <link rel="stylesheet" href="https://js.arcgis.
         com/4.4/esri/css/main.css"/>
8        <link rel="stylesheet" href="styles/main.css"/>
9        <script src="dojoConfig.js"></script>
10       <script src="https://js.arcgis.com/4.6"></script>
11     </head>
12     <body>
13       <div id="mainDiv">
14       </div>
15     </body>
16   </html>
```

© Rene Rubalcava 2017
R. Rubalcava, *Introducing ArcGIS API 4 for JavaScript*,
https://doi.org/10.1007/978-1-4842-3282-8_2

Here is the dojoConfig.js file:

```
1   var locationPath = window.location.pathname.replace
    (/\/[^\/]+$/, '/');
2   window.dojoConfig = {
3     deps: ['app/main'],
4     packages: [{
5       name: 'app',
6       location: locationPath + '/app',
7       main: 'main'
8     }]
9   };
```

Here is the first sample JavaScript file, app/main.js:

```
1   import Map from "esri/Map";
2   import SceneView from "esri/views/SceneView";
3
4   const map = new Map({ basemap: "topo" });
5   const view = new SceneView({
6     container: "mainDiv",
7     map,
8     center: [-118.182, 33.913],
9     scale: 836023
10  });
```

That's all you need to get a simple SceneView ready to go. You now
have an interactive 3D map you can work with.

How About That dojoConfig?

Let's talk briefly about how dojoConfig works in your development
environment. For most of the samples in this book, I'll assume you are using
the content delivery network (CDN) version of the ArcGIS API for JavaScript.

What's happening with this `locationPath`?

```
1  var locationPath = window.location.pathname.replace
   (/\/[^\/]+$/, '/');
```

Assume your application is hosted at `http://localhost/apps/myapplication`. The `location.pathname` would be `/apps/myapplication`. The regular expression `/\/[^\/]+$/` is going to turn it into `/apps/`. What you want to do is create a *package* for your application, which is basically a way for you to namespace your code into its own package to distinguish it from the dependencies.

```
1  window.dojoConfig = {
2    ...
3    packages: [{
4      name: 'app',
5      location: locationPath + '/app',
6      main: 'main'
7    }]
8  };
```

This is creating a package called app, and you are letting Dojo from the ArcGIS CDN know that the app is at `/apps/app` on your host and not the CDN. If you didn't do this, Dojo would try looking for an app package on the CDN where it does not exist. You are also saying that the app package has an entry point in a module called `main`.

```
1  window.dojoConfig = {
2    deps: ['app/main'],
3    ...
4  };
```

By stating `deps: ['app/main']` is a dependency of the project, the `app/main` module will automatically load when the application starts. You can actually list any modules that need to load before your application starts in this array.

7

You can read more about dojoConfig at https://dojotoolkit.org/
documentation/tutorials/1.10/dojo_config/.

AMD and Packages

I want to stress that you should write your code in ES6. This is to simplify
how you actually write your code; in addition, for me at least, it lets me
forget that I'm actually working with the Asynchronous Module Definition[1]
for my code. The ES6 code you write will be turned into ES5-compatible
AMD modules using a compiler such as BabelJS.[2] At the end of the day,
though, your code will still be AMD, and thus you should know a little bit
about it and packages.

AMD

When you write code such as this:

```
1   import Map from "esri/Map";
2   import SceneView from "esri/views/SceneView";
3
4   const map = new Map({ basemap: "topo" });
5   const view = new SceneView({
6       container: "mainDiv",
7       map,
8       center: [-118.182, 33.913],
9       scale: 836023
10  });
```

---

[1]https://github.com/amdjs/amdjs-api/blob/master/AMD.md
[2]https://babeljs.io/

Babel will compile it something more like this:

```
1    define(["exports", "module", "esri/Map", "esri/views/
     SceneView"], function(exports\
2    ts, module , _esriMap, _esriviewsSceneView) {
3
4      function _interopRequireDefault(obj) { return obj &&
       obj.__esModule ? obj : {\
5    'default': obj }; }
6
7      var _Map = _interopRequireDefault(_esriMap);
8      var _SceneView = _interopRequireDefault
       (_esriviewsSceneView);
9
10     var map = new Map["default"]({ basemap: "topo" });
11     var view = new SceneView["default"]({
12       container: "mainDiv",
13       map,
14       center: [-118.182, 33.913],
15       scale: 836023
16     });
17
18   });
```

Don't let all this code throw you off. The amount of code has to do with ES6 modules[3] and the import[4] statement. When you write import Map from "esri/Map";, it is assumed that the source code exports a default Object that actually points to the Map module. However, we still live in a

---

[3]http://jsmodules.io/
[4]https://developer.mozilla.org/en-US/docs/Web/JavaScript/Reference/
Statements/import

world where not everyone is writing ES6 code and the module system is not yet implemented in any browsers natively. So, you still need to account for some mixing and matching. That's what this output code does.

In AMD, you create modules with a `define` method. The first argument is an array that lists any other dependencies. The second argument is a function that returns the actual code for this module.

As I said earlier, though, if you write your code in ES6 and let the compiler create your AMD modules, you don't need to worry too much about some of these details. You should be aware of them, but don't let them weigh you down.

For more details, I'll direct you to the Dojo documentation for AMD modules.[5]

Packages

One area of confusion I have seen come up quite a bit is the idea of packages. Don't worry, it's something I was initially confused about when I first started out with AMD. Right now, you do not need to worry too much about packages, that is, until you decide that you want *build* your application. At that point, you should really learn what a package is.

A *package* is essentially a namespace similar to something like Java.[6] In the ArcGIS API for JavaScript 4, `esri` is a package and so is `dojo`. This means that `esri/Map` is a module in the `esri` package. When you write your own application code, you will typically create an `app` package. This lets you reference your own modules under the `app` package.

---

[5]https://dojotoolkit.org/documentation/tutorials/1.10/modules/index. html

[6]https://en.wikipedia.org/wiki/Java_package

So, your folder with source code may look like this:

```
1   src
2     ├── app
3          ├── /widgets
4          ├── /services
```

If you are working with the Bower[7] release of the ArcGIS API for JavaScript 4, you would ideally have all other packages in the same folder.

```
1   src
2     ├── app
3     ├── dgrid
4     ├── dijit
5     ├── dojo
6     ├── dojox
7     ├── dstore
8     ├── moment
9     ├── esri
```

This lets you easily organize your code and also lets the Dojo build tools[8] know what packages you are using.

There may be a need for you to use a library that is built using Universal Module Definition (UMD). In this case, the Dojo build system will recognize that you are trying to load something that looks like an AMD module but isn't quite an AMD module. You can let the Dojo build know how to load this package in the packages property of your build profile.

---

[7]http://bower.io/
[8]https://dojotoolkit.org/documentation/tutorials/1.10/build/

Let's take the moment library used in the API as an example. If you are going to do a custom local build using the Bower release of the API, you will want to make this small adjustment to your build profile:

```
1    packages: [
2      'app',
3      'dijit',
4      'dojo',
5      'dojox',
6      'dstore',
7      'dgrid',
8      'esri', {
9        name: 'moment',
10        location: 'moment',
11        main: 'moment',
12        trees: [
13          // don't bother with .hidden, tests, min, src, and
             templates
14          [".", ".", /(\/\.)|(~$)|(test|txt|src|min|templates)/]
15        ],
16        resourceTags: {
17          amd: function(filename, mid){
18            return /\.js$/.test(filename);
19          }
20        }
21      }
22    ]
```

In this case, you are defining a moment package by defining the name, location, and main properties. This is similar to how you defined the app package earlier. However, for this package, you are defining a resourceTags property. This property tells the Dojo build system, via a regular expression, that all .js files are AMD modules. You also add a trees property, which tells the Dojo build system to ignore hidden files, test directories, minified files, and more files you don't want the Dojo build system to try to build. These are the steps you would want to use to define a package for UMD files so they can be properly loaded into the Dojo build system.

Normally, these properties are defined in a JavaScript file inside your package folder. This file can be called anything you want, but it typically is called something like app.profile.js and will look like this:

```
1   var profile = (function () {
2     return {
3       resourceTags: {
4         amd: function (filename, mid) {
5           return /\.js$/.test(filename);
6         }
7       }
8     };
9   })();
```

There are other options you could add here, which can be found in the documentation.[9]

You can let the Dojo build system know how to find your package profile via the package.json file.

```
1   {
2       "name": "app",
3       "description": "My Application Package.",
4       "version": "1.0",
5       "dojoBuild": "app.profile.js"
6   }
```

---

[9]https://dojotoolkit.org/documentation/tutorials/1.10/build/

The Dojo build system will look for the `dojoBuild` property in the `package.json` file to figure out how to load your AMD package via the defined settings.

Summary

In this short chapter, I covered how to set up a basic application and define a `dojoConfig` object. You learned about the AMD loader as well as how to define AMD packages and how they are used in creating custom builds of the API using the Dojo build system. With this thorough understanding of packages, let's move on to some concepts of the ArcGIS API 4 for JavaScript.

CHAPTER 3

Maps and Views

The newest version of the ArcGIS API creates maps differently than
version 3.*x*.

```
1   import Map from "esri/Map";
2   import SceneView from "esri/views/SceneView";
3
4   const map = new Map({ basemap: "topo" });
5   const view = new SceneView({
6     container: "mainDiv",
7     map,
8     center: [-118.182, 33.913],
9     scale: 836023
10  });
```

There is now a distinct difference between the map (and the layers
that comprise a map) and how that map data is displayed. You can now
think of the map as the data source and think of the view as the visual
representation of the map.

You can see what this relationship looks like in Figure 3-1.

© Rene Rubalcava 2017
R. Rubalcava, *Introducing ArcGIS API 4 for JavaScript*,
https://doi.org/10.1007/978-1-4842-3282-8_3

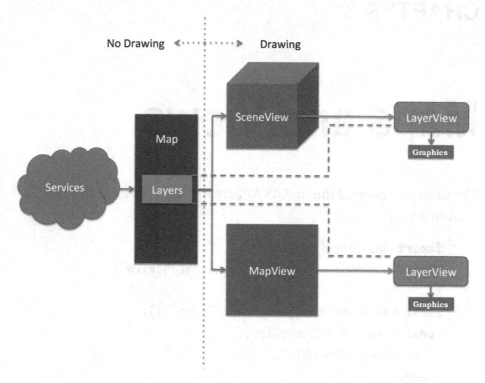

Figure 3-1. *Map-view relationship*

In Figure 3-1, you can see that the map is a container for various spatial services. This same map can now be displayed in a MapView, which is a 2D representation of the data, or a SceneView, which is a 3D representation of the data. Each of these views is responsible for how the data is visually displayed.

This means some features you may have taken for granted in the 3.*x* API, such as accessing the graphics directly on a FeatureLayer, are no longer available. This is because one view could display 10 features from a layer, while another view could display 100 features from the same layer. As you can see in Figure 3-1, each layer in a view is represented as a LayerView. You can get the LayerView of a view by using view. whenLayerView(sourceLayer). This will return a promise of the LayerView when it is complete. By doing so, you can get access to the actual graphics that are displayed in a view.

This separation of the map and views is a powerful new concept introduced in the ArcGIS API for JavaScript 4. With this feature, you could create a dozen different maps with different services without having to load all the data for them ahead of time until you attach a map to a view. This allows you to treat the map as a pure data source in your application that has access to the layers without even having to display a map.

WebMaps

Working with WebMap objects in version 4 of the API has never been easier. You can search for a variety of WebMaps in the ArcGIS gallery.[1]

To create a WebMap, you simply need to have an id value for the item in the portal.

```
1   import MapView from "esri/views/MapView";
2   import WebMap from "esri/WebMap";
3
4   const webmap = new WebMap({
5     portalItem: {
6       id: "2dfaf8bdb45a4dcf8511a849e4583873"
7     }
8   });
9
10  const view = new MapView({
11    map: webmap,
12    container: "viewDiv"
13  });
```

---

[1]www.arcgis.com/home/gallery.html

That is it. That's all you have to do to load the WebMap object into your application. But because the map is just a container of data, you can access the WebMap data before you display it on the page.

Say, for example, that you wanted to adjust the definitionExpression of a layer in the WebMap object before it's displayed. You could do something like this:

```
1   // http://jsbin.com/lodihu/4/edit?html,output
2   const webmap = new WebMap({
3     portalItem: {
4       id: "2dfaf8bdb45a4dcf8511a849e4583873"
5     }
6   });
7
8   webmap.load().then(() => {
9     const layer = webmap.layers.find({ id } => {
10      return id.indexOf("CensusTractPoliticalAffiliation
        Totals") > -1;
11    });
12    layer.definitionExpression = "TOTPOP_CY > 10000"
13    const view = new MapView({
14      map: webmap,
15      container: "viewDiv"
16    });
17  });
```

That right there is pretty cool. Notice how you have to call the load() method of the WebMap object. This is because when the WebMap is initialized, the data is not prefetched. It's only when a WebMap is added to a view does it load the data needed to display it. By calling the load() method, you are asking the WebMap to *please load your data* because you want to use it for whatever reason. This has the added benefit of letting you create multiple WebMap objects and passing them to the view as needed.

```
1   const webmapids = [
2     "e691172598f04ea8881cd2a4adaa45ba",
3     "2dfaf8bdb45a4dcf8511a849e4583873"
4   ];
5
6   // create an array of WebMaps
7   const webmaps = webmapids.map(webmapid => {
8     return new WebMap({
9       portalItem: {
10        id: webmapid
11      }
12    });
13  });
```

You can then keep these WebMap objects sitting around until you actually need them and want to use them in a view. It is also possible to switch the map of the view during runtime.

It should be noted that in the initial release of 4, not all layers and renderers are supported in the WebMap as of yet, but full support is currently in progess. Any layer that is not supported will be defined as UnsupportedLayer. There is also a layer type called UnknownLayer, which is used if a layer type cannot be determined. This layer is there in case new layer types are added in the future.

LayerViews

Since the map is simply a container of data and layers and the view is responsible for displaying that data, the way you interact with that data has changed. In the 3.x version of the ArcGIS API for JavaScript, you could access the graphics in a FeatureLayer directly from the layer. In version 4 of the API, the graphics are contained in the view, more precisely in the LayerView object, which is the views representation of the layer.

You can get access to the layer as shown here:

```
1   view.whenLayerView(layer).then((layerView)=>{
2       // Do something with the LayerView
3   });
```

Once you have the LayerView and you want to interact with the features being displayed from a FeatureLayer, you can gain access to them via a method called queryFeatures.

```
1   view.whenLayerView(layer).then((layerView)=>{
2       // make sure the layeView is done drawing the graphics
3       watchUtils.whenTrueOnce(layerView, "updating", ()=>{
4           layerView.queryFeatures().then((graphics)=>{
5               // Do something with the Graphics
6           });
7       });
8   });
```

There are a handful of other useful query methods you can use on a FeatureLayer LayerView.

- queryExtent: Returns the extent of the features in the LayerView

- queryFeatureCount: Returns a count of the features in the LayerView

- queryObjectIds: Returns an array of ObjectIds, which is pretty useful to do some more query tasks against the REST API

These are all useful methods if you want to create a custom widget that can interact with the features being displayed.

Layers

Retrieving the layers in the WebMap is easy to do. To access the layers on the map, you can simply retrieve them from the map.layers property. This property will provide you with the operational layers of the map, which means no basemaps. If you want all the layers, including the basemap, you can use the map.allLayers property. This is a much simpler API than the 3.x version.

If you only care about the basemap, you can get that via the map.basemap property.

To reiterate, the views and the LayerViews are what actually draw the data for the map. They control the display of graphics, the extent, and any other visual properties. The map and layers are containers of that data. They are the models for your map, which means they can be treated like models in your application development. The map and the layer can be used as a data source for charts or tables or any other type of custom component that may not even have a map to display. That's a powerful feature of the API.

There are a handful of layers available in the API, and each serves a different purpose. You can read more details about each type of layer in the API documentation, but these are some of the more common layers:

- GraphicsLayer
- FeatureLayer

21

- `MapImageLayer`
- `SceneLayer`
- `VectorTileLayer`

GraphicsLayer

The `GraphicsLayer` is probably the simplest layer you can work with. As the name suggests, it simply contains graphics that are displayed on the map.

Note   If you are familiar with the `GraphicsLayer` from the 3.*x* version of the ArcGIS API for JavaScript, one main difference with the `GraphicsLayer` in version 4 is that it does not support a renderer. You would need to define the symbology per graphic instead of on the layer. This is because the `GraphicsLayer` can support graphics with different geometry types. This greatly simplifies creating basic graphics to display on the map.

Initializing a `GraphicsLayer` is fairly simple.

```
1   const graphicsLayer = new GraphicsLayer({
2       graphics: [graphic1, graphic2, graphic3]
3   });
```

You can add graphics to the `GraphicsLayer` via a couple of methods.

```
1   // add a single graphic
2   graphicsLayer.add(graphic);
3   // add an array of graphics
4   graphicsLayer.addMany([graphic1, graphic2, graphic3]);
```

Since you can't set up a renderer or popup template for a GraphicsLayer, you'll need to define the symbology and popups on a per-graphic basis.

```javascript
1   // create a graphic
2   let graphic = new Graphic({
3     attributes: {
4       id: 1,
5       city: "Los Angeles"
6     },
7     geometry: { type: "point", x: xValue, y: yValue },
8     symbol: { type: "simple-marker",
9       style: 'circle',
10      color: 'red',
11      size: 10,
12      outline: {
13        color: 'rgba(255, 255, 255, 0.5)'
14        width: 4
15      }
16    },
17    popupTemplate: {
18      title: "My Awesome Graphic!",
19      content: "{*}" // display all fields
20    }
21  });
22
23  // add it to graphicsLayer
24  graphicsLayer.add(graphic);
```

Popups will be covered in more detail in a later chapter.

If you need more robust support for your graphics, in particular using a renderer and popups, you'll want to use a FeatureLayer. The GraphicsLayer is ideal as simply a bag of miscellaneous graphics.

FeatureLayer

FeatureLayers are probably the most versatile and widely used layer type in the ArcGIS platform. There are a few different ways you can initialize a FeatureLayer.

```
1    // Create via URL
2    const featureLayer = new FeatureLayer({
3      url: "http://services6.arcgis.com/m3L8QUZ93HeaQzKv/
         arcgis/rest/services/BeerAn\
4    dBurgerJoints/FeatureServer/0"
5    });
6
7    // Create via a Portal item
8    const featureLayer = new FeatureLayer({
9      portalItem: {
10       id: "b126510e440744169943fd8ccc9b0c4e"
11     }
12   });
```

By initializing a FeatureLayer via one of these two methods, the layer is now bound to a remote service. The same way you can query the LayerView of a FeatureLayer, you can query directly against the FeatureLayer to find the features, ObjectIds, or extent of a FeatureLayer.

You can also create a FeatureLayer via a FeatureCollection, although it has been simplified since the 3.*x* version of the API.

```
1    const featureLayer = new FeatureLayer({
2      objectIdField: "item_id",
```

```
3      geometryType: "point",
4      // Define the fields of the graphics in the FeatureLayer
5      fields: [{
6        name: "item_id",
7        alias: "Item ID",
8        type: "oid"
9      }, {
10       name: "description",
11       alias: "Description",
12       type: "string"
13     }, {
14       name: "title",
15       alias: "Title",
16       type: "string"
17     }],
18     // Define a renderer for the layer
19     renderer: {
20       type: "simple",
21       symbol: {
       type: "simple-marker",
22         style: 'circle',
23         color: 'red',
24         size: 10,
25         outline: {
26           color: 'rgba(255, 255, 255, 0.5)'
27           width: 4
28         }
29       }
30     },
31     popupTemplate: {
32       title: "{title}",
33       content: "{description}"
```

```
34    },
35    // This is a collection of Graphics
36    source: [graphic1, graphic2, graphic3]
37  });
```

What you are doing here is defining the source for a FeatureLayer manually. This basically passes along a collection of graphics and defines the renderer for those graphics, as well as the fields and popup. The benefit here is the ability to use a single renderer for multiple graphics as well as a single popup. You will also have the ability to query against this FeatureLayer the same way you could query a FeatureLayer tied to a remote service.

Now, maybe you want to update the source features in a FeatureLayer. You can do this in the following manner:

```
1  const graphicOfInterest = featureLayer.source.find(x =>
   x.attributes.OBJECTID ==\
2  = oid);
3  const target = graphicOfInterest.clone();
4  const target.geometry = updatedGeometry;
5  featureLayer.source.remove(graphicOfInterest);
6  featureLayer.source.add(target);
```

This lets you update individual graphics in the FeatureLayer source. This comes in handy if you want to display updated GPS data or maybe change the symbology for individual features.

MapImageLayer

The MapImageLayer was previously known as the ArcGISDynamicMapServiceLayer. It lets you load dynamic map services into your application, which, unlike tiled image services, loads a single image for the entire map extent instead of many tiles.

It's a fairly simple layer to work with. You can even define what sublayers are visible in the MapImageLayer, which used to be a cumbersome task. Working with sublayers is now much easier.

```
1   const layer = new MapImageLayer({
2     url: "https://sampleserver6.arcgisonline.com/arcgis/
      rest/services/USA/MapServe\
3   r",
4     sublayers: [{
5       id: 0,
6       visible: true
7     }, {
8       id: 1,
9       visible: true
10    }, {
11      id: 2,
12      visible: true
13    }, {
14      id: 3,
15      visible: false
16    }]
17  });
```

You can simply define the visibility of each sublayer in the sublayers property of the MapImageLayer. You could even take it a step further and provide a definitionExpression for individual sublayers.

```
1   let layer = new MapImageLayer({
2     url: "https://sampleserver6.arcgisonline.com/arcgis/
rest/services/USA/MapServe\
3   r",
```

```
 4    sublayers: [{
 5      id: 0,
 6      visible: true
 7    }, {
 8      id: 1,
 9      visible: true
10    }, {
11      id: 2,
12      visible: true,
13      // provide a definitionExpression
14      definitionExpression: "pop2000 > 1000000"
15    }, {
16      id: 3,
17      visible: false
18    }]
19  });
```

This will now pass a definitionExpression for the sublayer to the dynamic map service when it requests the image. This follows along with the theme of the entire version 4 of the ArcGIS API for JavaScript to provide a simpler API. I fully expect people to implement the utility of the MapImageLayer in their applications with this easier-to-use API.

With version 4 of the ArcGIS API 4 for JavaScript, the sublayers you define will be the only sublayers used in the MapImageLayer. This is incredibly useful if you are working with a map service that contains hundreds of layers, which I have personally seen far too many times.

You can also define a popupTemplate[2] and even a renderer[3] per sublayer.

_____

[2]https://developers.arcgis.com/javascript/latest/api-reference/esri-PopupTemplate.html

[3]https://developers.arcgis.com/javascript/latest/api-reference/esri-renderers-Renderer.html

```
1   const layer = new MapImageLayer({
2     url: "https://sampleserver6.arcgisonline.com/arcgis/
      rest/services/Census/MapSe\
3   rver",
4     sublayers: [
5     {
6       id: 3,
7       visible: true,
8       renderer: {type: "simple",
9         symbol: { type: "simple-fill",
10          style: "solid",
11          color: "dodgerblue",
12          outline: {
13            width: 0.5,
14            color: "white"
15          }
16        },
17        label: "State boundaries"
18      },
19      opacity: 0.5
20    },
21    {
22      id: 2,
23      visible: true,
24      popupTemplate: {
25          title: "{NAME}",
26          content: [
27          {
28            fieldInfos: [
29              {
30                fieldName: "POP2000",
31                visible: true,
```

```
32            label: "Population for year 2000",
33            format: {
34              places: 0,
35              digitSeparator: true
36            }
37          },
38          {
39            fieldName: "POP2007",
40            visible: true,
41            label: "Population for year 2007",
42            format: {
43              places: 0,
44              digitSeparator: true
45            }
46          }
47        ]
48      },
49      {
50        type: "media",
51        mediaInfos: [
52          {
53            title: "<b>Population</b>",
54            type: "column-chart",
55            caption: "",
56            value: {
57              theme: "Grasshopper",
58              fields: [ "POP2000", "POP2007" ],
59              normalizeField: null,
60              tooltipField: null
61            }
62          }
63        ]
```

```
64              }
65          ]
66          }
67      },
68      {
69          id: 0,
70          visible: true,
71          definitionExpression: "POP2000 > 100000"
72      }]
73  });
```

This is incredibly powerful as you can now work with map services *almost* as easily as a FeatureService. The ability to define a custom renderer for dynamic map services has been available for quite some time in the 3.*x* version of the API, and it's been available as part of the ArcGIS Server map service for some time as well. What is new, starting with the version 4 of the ArcGIS API for JavaScript, is that it has simplified the API for developers to more easily take advantage of this feature. The addition of being able to define popups per sublayer just adds to the utility of the MapImageLayer, and I'm not afraid to say that I think this is now my personal favorite layer to work with as part of the API.

There is even more you can do with the MapImageLayer via query tables and table joins if you have that data available via your services. Check out the documentation[4] for those details and bask in the glory of the MapImageLayer.

---

[4]https://developers.arcgis.com/javascript/latest/api-reference/esri-layers-MapImageLayer.html

CSVLayer

The CSVLayer[5] is incredibly useful in the ArcGIS API 4 for JavaScript to represent tabular data spatially.

As long as the CSV file has fields of the following names with coordinates, it can convert the file for you:

- *Longitude field names*: lon, lng, long, longitude, x, xcenter, longitude83, longdecdeg, POINT-X

- *Latitude field names*: lat, latitude, y, ycenter, latitude83, latdecdeg, POINT-Y

If your CSV file does not conform to that format, you can specify custom latitude and longitude field names using the latitudeField and longitudeField properties of the CSVLayer.

```
1   let csvLayer = new CSVLayer({
2     url: "http://ontheinternet/mydata.csv",
3     copyright: "Please provide a copyright for the data"
4   });
```

Note that depending on where the CSV file is originating, you may need to provide a proxyRule in your application.

```
1   urlUtils.addProxyRule({
2     urlPrefix: "ontheinternet",
3     proxyUrl: "/proxy/"
4   });
```

---

[5]https://developers.arcgis.com/javascript/latest/api-reference/esri-layers-CSVLayer.html

SceneLayer

A key component of working with 3D maps is the SceneLayer.
SceneLayers allow you to load a scene service[6] into your 3D mapping
applications. Once you have a SceneLayer, it's fairly straightforward to add
it to your 3D map via the SceneView.

```
1   const sceneLayer = new SceneLayer({
2     url: "http://scene.arcgis.com/arcgis/rest/services/
      Hosted/Building_Boston/Scen\
3   eServer/layers/0";
4   });
5
6   const map = new Map({
7     basemap: "streets",
8     ground: "world-elevation",
9     layers: [sceneLayer]
10  });
11
12  const view = new SceneView({
13    container: "viewDiv",
14    map: map,
15    scale: 50000000,
16    center: [-101.17, 21.78]
17  });
```

I'll cover 3D visualizations and the SceneView in later chapters, but
all you really need to know is that adding a SceneLayer to your map is
identical to how you add other layers.

---

[6]http://server.arcgis.com/en/server/latest/publish-services/windows/
scene-services.htm

VectorTileLayer

Vector tiles are pretty interesting. Mapbox released the Vector Tile Specification[7] not too long ago, and it has proven to be incredibly versatile. The file size for vector tiles is small, which allows for some high-resolution basemaps and efficient caching of data. Vector tiles basically store vector data in a compact format that allows for a flexible styling of those vector features in the browser. This is as opposed to creating tiled images of that data that cannot be styled in the browser.

You will typically have a single service that provides all the vector tiles for your applications. You can, however, load different styles for those services so you can load the same data but with a different look.

When you initialize a `VectorTileLayer`, you do it the same way you do every other layer.

```
1   const tileLyr = new VectorTileLayer({
2     url: "https://www.arcgis.com/sharing/rest/content/items/
      f96366254a564adda1dc46\
3   8b447ed956/resources/styles/root.json"
4   });
```

If you look at the URL used to initialize a `VectorTileLayer`, you can see that it actually points to a style file instead of a specific layer ID. The URL you point to is `resources/styles/root.json`. This is actually just a style file that defines how the `VectorTileLayer` should be styled when it is rendered on the map.

You can actually switch the style of your `VectorTileLayer` during runtime by using the `loadStyle()` method, as in `vectorTileLayer.loadStyle(myNewStyleObject)`.

---

[7]https://github.com/mapbox/vector-tile-spec

Vector tiles are a treat for cartographers because vector tiles provide flexibility to design some very stylish and impactful basemaps. You can test the styling the ArcGIS vector tile basemaps via this vector tile style editor: `https://github.com/Esri/arcgis-vectortile-style-editor`.

Recently, the ArcGIS API 4 for JavaScript started using its own implementation for vector tiles. This new implementation allows the API to render vector tiles of different projections and makes them usable in a 3D environment; however, the current implementation does not support Mapbox tiles.

Vector tiles provide incredibly crisp and good-looking maps. It's important to know that vector tiles make use of WebGL,[8] which relies on your video card and browser support. If you see some artifacts or you notice smoke coming out of your laptop, you may want to look into upgrading your video card drivers.

GroupLayer

The GroupLayer[9] is an interesting layer. It doesn't pull data from a web service; however, it will allow you to group your layers together. The layers don't need to be of the same type; you can group a GraphicsLayer with a TiledLayer, and everything will simply work. A use case where this could be useful is controlling the visibility of multiple similar or related FeatureLayers. Let's take a look at the following sample:

```
1  import Map from "esri/Map";
2  import MapView from "esri/views/MapView";
3  import FeatureLayer from "esri/layers/FeatureLayer";
```

---

[8]`https://developer.mozilla.org/en-US/docs/Web/API/WebGL_API`
[9]`https://developers.arcgis.com/javascript/latest/api-reference/esri-layers-GroupLayer.html`

```
4    import GroupLayer from "esri/layers/GroupLayer";
5
6    const URL = "http://tmservices1.esri.com/arcgis/rest/
     services/LiveFeeds/NOAA_sto\
7    rm_reports/MapServer";
8    const titles = [
9      "NOAA HAIL Storm Reports (24 hours)",
10     "NOAA TORNADO Storm Reports (24 hours)",
11     "NOAA WIND Storm Reports (24 hours)",
12     "NOAA TORNADO Storm Reports (past week)"
13   ];
14   const layers = [0, 1, 2, 3].map((index, idx) => {
15     return new FeatureLayer({
16       url: `${URL}/${index}`,
17       outFields: ["*"],
18       popupTemplate: {
19         title: titles[idx],
20         content: "{*}"
21       }
22     });
23   });
24   const groupLayer = new GroupLayer({ layers });
25   const map = new Map({
26     basemap: "streets",
27     layers: [groupLayer]
28   });
29   const view = new MapView({
30     container: "viewDiv",
31     map,
32     center: [-98.648, 36.374],
33     zoom: 5,
```

```
34    ui: {
35      components: ["zoom", "attribution", "compass"]
36    }
37  });
38  view.then(() => {
39    const btn = document.createElement("div");
40    btn.className = "esri-button esri-widget-button
      esri-interactive esri-icon-fea\
41  ture-layer";
42    btn.title = "Toggle Storm Data";
43    view.ui.add(btn, "top-right");
44    // toggle layer visibility of GroupLayer
45    btn.addEventListener("click", () => {
46      groupLayer.visible = !groupLayer.visible;
47    });
48  });
```

What you are able to do here is toggle the visibility of the GroupLayer. When you do this, the visibility of the grouped layers is also toggled.

Portal API

While using the ArcGIS API 4 for JavaScript, with WebMaps, WebScenes, and even layers, the underlying API that powers most of this is the Portal API. The Portal API consists of a set of modules, ranging from the Portal class itself[10] to PortalItem.[11] You can utilize the Portal API to build a robust data explorer of your portal, but it's also used in more subtle ways throughout the API.

---

[10]https://developers.arcgis.com/javascript/latest/api-reference/esri-portal-Portal.html

[11]https://developers.arcgis.com/javascript/latest/api-reference/esri-portal-PortalItem.html

37

```
1    const webmap = new WebMap({
2      portalItem: {
3        id: webmapid
4      }
5    });
6
7    const webscene = new WebScene({
8      portalItem: {
9        id: sceneid
10     }
11   });
```

These examples use *autocasting*, which is covered in Chapter 4.

Both WebMap and WebScene utilize the Portal API under the hood to build their respective maps and scenes. For example, a WebMap may consist of three layers from a portal. Each layer is referenced by its own portal item ID. When you load a WebMap by its ID, the Portal API is used to load that WebMap and then recursively load each layer item referenced by an ID or possibly simply a URL. The beauty of this is that when a map and even a layer is created, those resources are not immediately loaded. What this means for you as a developer is that you could initialize a group of WebMaps or layers without loading all their required resources and instead load that data only as needed. This is incredibly efficient for development purposes.

Let's look at what an application loading portal items may look like (Figure 3-2).

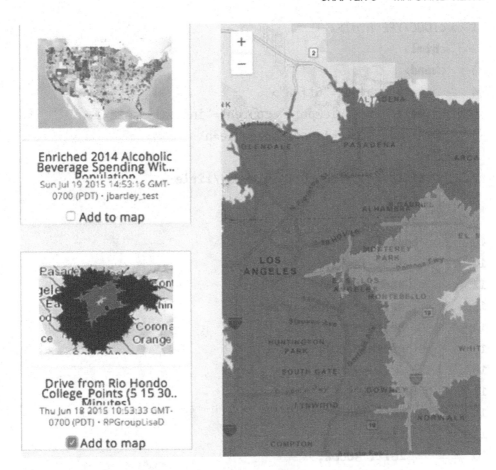

Figure 3-2. *Adding layers via portal items*

You'll use `calcite-bootstrap`[12] to help you style this app because it already has styling for nice-looking portal item cards built in. You can modify an existing sample[13] to be a bit more explicit about working portal items and the generated layers.

---

[12]https://github.com/Esri/calcite-bootstrap

[13]https://developers.arcgis.com/javascript/latest/sample-code/ portalitem-dragndrop/index.html

```
1    <!DOCTYPE html>
2    <html>
3    <head>
4      <meta charset="utf-8">
5      <meta name="viewport" content="initial-scale=1,
     maximum-scale=1,user-scalable=n\
6    o">
7      <title>Fun with Portal Items</title>
8      <style>
9        html,
10       body {
11         font-family: sans-serif;
12         padding: 0;
13         margin: 0 !important;
14         height: 100%;
15         width: 100%;
16       }
17       #viewDiv {
18         position: absolute;
19         right: 0;
20         left: 300px;
21         top: 0;
22         bottom: 0;
23       }
24       #itemDiv {
25         position: absolute;
26         left: 0;
27         top: 0;
28         bottom: 0;
29         width: 300px;
30         overflow-y: auto;
31       }
```

```
32      .description {
33        margin: 0 auto;
34        width: 100%;
35        padding: 20px;
36      }
37      .card h6 {
38        margin: 0 !important;
39      }
40    </style>
41    <link href="http://esri.github.io/calcite-bootstrap/
      assets/css/calcite-bootstr\
42  ap-open.min.css" rel="stylesheet">
43    <link rel="stylesheet" href="https://js.arcgis.com/4.6/
      esri/css/main.css">
44    <script>
45      window.dojoConfig = {
46        deps: ['app/main'],
47        packages: [{
48          name: 'app',
49          location: window.location.pathname.replace(/\/
            [^\/]+$/, ''); + 'app',
50          main: 'main'
51        }]
52      };
53    </script>
54    <script src="https://js.arcgis.com/4.6/"></script>
55  </head>
56  <body>
57    <div id="itemDiv">
58      <label class="description">Add layer items to
        Map</label>
```

```
59        <ul class="cards-list">
60        </ul>
61      </div>
62      <div id="viewDiv"></div>
63      </div>
64    </body>
65    </html>
```

This is the code for the app/main.js file.

```
1     import Map from 'esri/Map';
2     import MapView from 'esri/views/MapView';
3     import Layer from  "esri/layers/Layer";
4     import PortalItem from "esri/portal/PortalItem";
5     import esriLang from "esri/core/lang";
6     import all from "dojo/promise/all";
7     import on from "dojo/on";
8
9     // create a card template to display Portal Item
      Information
10    const template = `
11    <li data-itemid="{id}">
12      <article class="card"><img src="{thumbnailUrl}"
      alt="Card Thumbnail">
13        <hr>
14        <h6>{title}</h6>
15        <ul class="card-info">
16          <li>{created}</li>
17          <li>{owner}</li>
18        </ul>
19        <div class="checkbox">
20          <label>
21            <input type="checkbox"> Add to map
```

```
22        </label>
23      </div>
24    </article>
25  </li>
26  `;
27  // Array of Portal Items for Layers
28  const layerItems = [
29    "a88018dc6c8045378f65b7abeb1d5a30",
30    "6df6df711e8f4b09bf7c1fcbae2afdd3",
31    "f1fca09035074e95a64c49548e79e625",
32    "d816e92c10bd4505bfcfbb761d5ac97d",
33    "ea7ff2ac9b4d49cdbe63dbf4ba2f21cd"
34  ];
35  const map = new Map({
36    basemap: "streets-navigation-vector"
37  });
38  const view = new MapView({
39    map,
40    container: "viewDiv",
41    zoom: 12,
42    center: [-118.1670, 34.0224]
43  });
44  // container to hold our cards
45  const $cardsList = document.querySelector(".cards-list");
46  view.then(() => {
47    // Create new PortalItem instances from our list
48    const portalItems = layerItems.map(id => (new
       PortalItem({ id }).load()));
49    // Use dojo/promise/all to wait for all
50    // PortalItem Promises to complete.
51    all(portalItems).then(items => {
```

```
52      let docFrag = document.createDocumentFragment();
53      // Iterate over each item to create a card for it
54      items.forEach(item => {
55        // esri/lang::substitute will create a new string
          using the PortalItem.
56        const card = esriLang.substitute(item, template);
57        const elem = document.createElement("div");
58        elem.innerHTML = card;
59        let layer;
60        // add listener for when checkbox is checked
61        on(elem, "input:click", ({ target }) => {
62          if (target.checked && !layer) {
63            if (item.isLayer) {
64              // This static method creates layers from
65              // Portal Items
66              Layer.fromPortalItem({
67                portalItem: item
68              }).then(function (lyr) {
69                // Now you can add the Layer to the map
70                layer = lyr;
71                map.add(lyr);
72                view.extent = item.extent;
73              });
74            }
75          }
76          else if (target.checked && layer) {
77            // Layer already created, just add it
78            map.add(layer);
79            view.extent = item.extent;
80          }
```

```
81          else {
82              // remove the layer if unchecked
83              map.remove(layer);
84          }
85      });
86      docFrag.appendChild(elem);
87    });
88    // Append the completed list to the page.
89    $cardsList.appendChild(docFrag);
90    docFrag = undefined;
91  });
92 });
```

For loading layers via a portal ID, you can use the static property
Layer.fromPortalItem(). All you need to do is pass in a PortalItem or
PortalItem-like object, and it will take care of the rest. It is important to
note that Layer.fromPortalItem() returns a promise with the generated
layer, so you will need to wait for the promise to complete and then you
can add the layer to the map.

```
1  Layer.fromPortalItem({
2    portalItem: {
3      id: layerPortalId
4    }
5  });
```

The Layer class will verify that the portal item is a layer and then
determine what type of layer it needs to be, such a TileLayer or
FeatureLayer.

Maybe you would like to build a simple explorer for your portal items
into an application. You could use the Portal API to query your portal items
and display the item information in your application (see Figure 3-3).

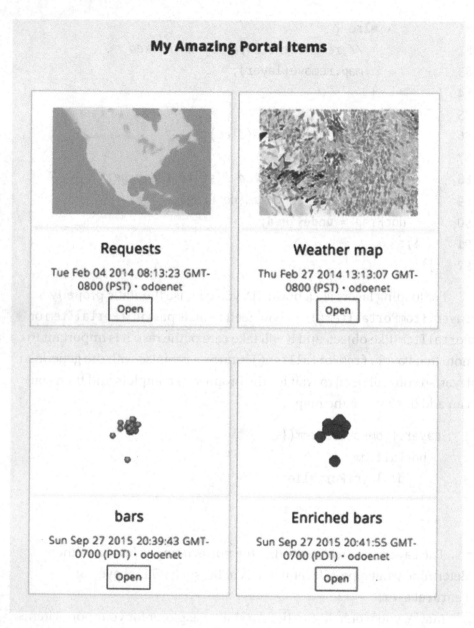

Figure 3-3. *Sample portal explorer*

Here is the basic HTML page for this application:

```
1   <!DOCTYPE html>
2   <html>
3   <head>
4     <meta charset="utf-8">
5     <meta name="viewport" content="initial-scale=1,
      maximum-scale=1,user-scalable=n\
6   o">
7     <title>Fun with Portal Items</title>
8     <style>
9       html,
10      body {
11        font-family: sans-serif;
12        padding: 0;
13        margin: 0 !important;
14        height: 100%;
15        width: 100%;
16      }
17      #viewDiv {
18        position: absolute;
19        right: 0;
20        left: 300px;
21        top: 0;
22        bottom: 0;
23      }
24      #itemDiv {
25        padding: 25px;
26        display: flex;
27        flex-direction: row;
28        flex-wrap: wrap;
29      }
```

```
30      .portal-item {
31        flex-grow: 4;
32      }
33      .item-link {
34        margin: 5px;
35      }
36      .description {
37        text-align: center;
38        margin: 0 auto;
39        width: 100%;
40        padding: 20px;
41      }
42      .card h6 {
43        height: 3rem !important;
44        margin: 0 !important;
45        padding: 0 !important;
46      }
47    </style>
48    <link href="http://esri.github.io/calcite-bootstrap/
      assets/css/calcite-bootstr\
49  ap-open.min.css" rel="stylesheet">
50    <link rel="stylesheet" href="https://js.arcgis.com/4.6/
      esri/css/main.css">
51    <script>
52      window.dojoConfig = {
53        deps: ['app/main'],
54        packages: [{
55          name: 'app',
56          location: window.location.pathname.replace(/\/
          [^\/]+$/, '') + 'app',
57          main: 'main'
58        }]
```

```
59        };
60    </script>
61    <script src="https://js.arcgis.com/4.6/"></script>
62    </head>
63    <body>
64      <label class="description">My Amazing Portal Items</label>
65      <div id="itemDiv" class="cards-list"></div>
66    </body>
67    </html>
```

You can write your application to load your own portal information.

```
1     import Portal from "esri/portal/Portal";
2     import PortalItem from "esri/portal/PortalItem";
3     import OAuthInfo from "esri/identity/OAuthInfo";
4     import esriId from "esri/identity/IdentityManager";
5     import PortalQueryParams from "esri/portal/
      PortalQueryParams";
6     import esriLang from "esri/core/lang";
7     import on from "dojo/on";
8
9     // create a card template to display Portal Item
      Information
10    const template = `
11    <div data-itemid="{id}">
12      <article class="card"><img src="{thumbnailUrl}"
        alt="Card Thumbnail">
13        <hr>
14        <h6>{title}</h6>
15        <ul class="card-info">
16          <li>{created}</li>
17          <li>{owner}</li>
18        </ul>
```

```
19        <div class="item-link">
20          <a class="btn btn-sm btn-default" href="https://
          {owner}.maps.arcgis.com/ho\
21   me/item.html?id={id}" target="_blank">Open</a>
22        </div>
23      </article>
24    </div>
25    `;
26
27   // container to hold our cards
28   const $cardsList = document.querySelector(".cards-list");
29   const info = new OAuthInfo({
30     appId: "zppZ53G093yZV7tG",
31     popup: false
32   });
33   // Add the OAuthInfo to IdentityManager
34   esriId.registerOAuthInfos([info]);
35   // now set up the Portal
36   const portal = new Portal({
37     // https://developers.arcgis.com/javascript/latest/api-
        reference/esri-portal-P\
38   ortal.html#authMode
39     authMode: "immediate"
40   });
41   // Will trigger a login if the user is not already
42   // logged in via this application
43   portal.load().then(() => {
44     const queryParams = new PortalQueryParams({
45       query: `owner:${portal.user.username}`,
46       sortField: "numViews",
47       sortOrder: "desc",
48       num: 20
```

```
49      });
50      return portal.queryItems(queryParams);
51   }).then(({ results }) => {
52      let docFrag = document.createDocumentFragment();
53      // Iterate over each item to create a card for it
54      results.forEach(item => {
55          // esri/lang::substitute will create a new string
          // using the PortalItem.
56          const card = esriLang.substitute(item, template);
57          const elem = document.createElement("div");
58          elem.className = "portal-item";
59          elem.innerHTML = card;
60          docFrag.appendChild(elem);
61      });
62      // Append the completed list to the page.
63      $cardsList.appendChild(docFrag);
64      docFrag = undefined;
65   });
```

What you are able to do here is use the Portal[14] module to get access
to your portal items. Then you can simply iterate over the portal items
and add nice little cards with descriptions and thumbnails for your portal
items, with links to open the actual item. This is a great way to be able
to get access to your portal items quickly if you want to use them in your
application.

---

[14]https://developers.arcgis.com/javascript/latest/api-reference/esri-
portal-Portal.html

Summary

In this chapter, I covered the relationship between maps and views and the benefits of having views manage the rendering pipeline of the data in the map. I also covered how LayerView allows you to access the features that are currently displayed in the view and the advantages of being able to query those features. You learned about the various layer types supported in the API and some of the new capabilities and functionality they provide. I also covered the new capabilities of the Portal API and the simplicity it provides for loading layers from a portal and also for searching for various portal items. These are core concepts in the API that you can build on to create awesome applications! In the next chapter, I will cover the core fundamentals of the API—essentially the building blocks for how the API is designed—that will let you take your skills to the next level.

CHAPTER 4

API Core Fundamentals

In the ArcGIS API 4 for JavaScript, there are a handful of fundamental concepts that make up how the API is built. If you get familiar with these core concepts, it will greatly benefit you when working with the API.

Accessors

An important addition to the ArcGIS API for JavaScript is the Accessor[1] module. It is located at `esri/core/Accessor`, which should tell you that it is a core part of the API. This is no mistake because most of the API is built on Accessors and their capabilities.

The Accessor module is loosely based on ES5 getters/setters[2] via the `Object.defineProperty`[3] method.

---

[1]https://developers.arcgis.com/javascript/latest/api-reference/esri-core-Accessor.html

[2]http://javascriptplayground.com/blog/2013/12/es5-getters-setters/

[3]https://developer.mozilla.org/en-US/docs/Web/JavaScript/Reference/Global_Objects/Object/defineProperty

Watching for Property Changes

What makes an Accessor interesting is that instead of listening for events to find out when changes have occurred on an object, you can simply watch for changes on the properties themselves.

```
1   // watching for events
2   widget.on("value-change", (val) => {
3       console.log(val);
4   });
5
6   // new method
7   widget.watch("value", (val) => {
8       console.log(val);
9   })
```

This also opens up the opportunity to watch for any value to change, not just changes that have events assigned to them. This is similar to how dojo/Stateful[4] works, except you don't need to use get/set methods.

```
1   // dojo/stateful
2   widget.set("value", newValue);
3
4   // Accessor
5   widget.value = newValue;
```

You can, however, still use the set method to set deep properties of an Accessor.

```
1   // update the property "view.map.basemap.title"
2   view.set("map.basemap.title", newTitle);
```

---

[4]https://dojotoolkit.org/reference-guide/1.10/dojo/Stateful.html

Or you can set multiple properties at once.

```
1  // update the property "view.map.basemap.title"
2  view.set({
3    constraints: {
4      minScale: 250000,
5      maxScale: 0
6    },
7    rotation: 45
8  });
```

You also have the ability to watch for nested property changes.

```
1  // update the property "view.map.basemap.title"
2  view.watch("map.basemap.title", (newValue) => /*handle
   result*/);
```

Every method returns a WatchHandle,[5] so you can stop listening to property changes via a remove method.

```
1  // update the property "view.map.basemap.title"
2  const handler = view.watch("map.basemap.title", (newValue)
   => /*handle result*/);
3  // at some point in the application remove the handler
4  function cleanup() {
5    handler.remove();
6  }
```

There is another great feature of being able to watch for property changes, which is the ability to watch for *multiple* properties to change.

---

[5]https://developers.arcgis.com/javascript/latest/api-reference/esri-core-Accessor.html#~WatchHandle

```
1    import Map from "esri/Map";
2    import MapView from "esri/views/MapView";
3
4    const map = new Map({
5      basemap: "streets"
6    });
7
8    const view = new MapView({
9      container: "viewDiv",
10     map: map,
11     zoom: 4,
12     center: [15, 65]
13   });
14
15   view.watch("center, scale", (value, oldValue,
     propertyName) => {
16     if (propertyName === "center") {
17       // Print the x & y of center
18       console.log(value.x, value.y);
19     } else {
20       // Print the scale value
21       console.log(value);
22     }
23   });
```

In this case, you're watching for both the center and scale properties of the view to change. When these changes occur, you just need to decide how to handle them. For this demo, you'll just print the results to the developer console. The flexibility of being able to watch for property changes in your application is a testament to the power that Accessors bring to the API.

Because the ability to watch for property changes is core to the API, there is a utility module provided to help you do that. You can find this utility in esri/core/watchUtils.[6] This comes in handy if you find yourself doing some conditional checks when watching for a property change.

```
1   view.watch("stationary", (value) => {
2     if (value) {
3       // do something when only true
4     }
5   });
```

That adds some cognitive overload, at least for me, that I would like to avoid. I only care about when the value is true, so I can use a utility for that.

```
1   watchUtils.whenTrue(view, "stationary", () => {
2     // do something
3   });
```

Let's look at a sample that will do a count of the number of points on the screen as you interact with the map.

Here is some sample code that shows how you might accomplish this:

```
1   import Map from "esri/Map";
2   import FeatureLayer from "esri/layers/FeatureLayer";
3   import watchUtils from "esri/core/watchUtils";
4   import SceneView from "esri/views/SceneView";
5   import QueryTask from "esri/tasks/QueryTask";
6   import Query from "esri/tasks/supports/Query";
7
8   const url = "http://services.arcgis.com/P3ePLMYs2RVChkJx/
    arcgis/rest/services/US\
```

---

[6]https://developers.arcgis.com/javascript/latest/api-reference/esri-core-watchUtils.html

```
 9    A_Major_Cities/FeatureServer/0";
10    const map = new Map({
11        basemap: "streets",
12        layers: [ new FeatureLayer({ url }) ]
13    }):
14    const query = new Query();
15    const queryTask = new QueryTask({ url });
16    const view = new SceneView({
17        container: "map",
18        map: map,
19        center: [-118.182, 33.913],
20        scale: 836023
21    });
22
23    query.watch("geometry", () =>{
24        qTask.executeForCount(query).then((count) =>{
25            document.getElementById("cityCount").innerText =
                count;
26        });
27    });
28
29    view.then(() =>{
30        watchUtils.whenTrue(view, "stationary", () =>{
31            query.geometry = view.extent;
32        });
33        watchUtils.whenFalse(view, "stationary", () =>{
34            document.getElementById("cityCount").innerText
                = "...";
35        });
36    });
```

watchUtils

As we have seen, watching for property changes is extremely useful in the API. Because your specific needs while watching for properties may differ based on your application needs, there is a helper you can use called watchUtils.[7]

Let's look at a few of the more interesting ones:

- watchUtils.init(): This is a utility that can come in handy when you need to grab the initial values of a property. Remember, when you are watching for property changes, you won't get notified until the property actually changes. This means you won't know what the initial values for many properties are unless you use this utility to watch for changes, *plus* get the initial value.

```
1   watchUtils.init(view, "stationary", (value,
       oldValue) => console.log(`New/Initia\
2   l value is "${value}" and Old value is
       "${oldValue}"`));
```

This will give you the initial value of the property, which is the default value, and all future updates like a regular watcher would. This is useful if you need the initial value to kick off an action in your application or display a value on the page but don't want to wait for the value to change.

---

[7]https://developers.arcgis.com/javascript/latest/api-reference/esri-core-watchUtils.html

- watchUtils.once(): As the name implies, this
  watch method is useful if you only care about
  watching for property changes once. This is also a
  subset of the watch helper methods that return a
  PromiseWatchHandle.[8] This means you can treat this
  watcher like any promise and even chain the results of
  this watcher in your application.

```
1   watchUtils.once(view, "camera").then(({ value,
    oldValue, propertyName, target })\
2     => {
3       return geometryEngineAsync.union([oldValue.
        position, value.position]);
4   }).then(positionMultiPoints => {
5     // store or continue using unioned points
6   });
```

As you can see, the ability to have a promise for
certain watch helpers can be useful.

- watchUtils.pausable(): I'm a big fan of this little
  helper. As the name advertises, this is a watcher you
  can pause and then simply resume as needed.

```
1   const handler = watchUtils.pausable(view,
    "center", updateComponentMethod);
2   // resize component, no need to update during
    animated resize
3   handler.pause();
4   // resize of component is done, resume updates
5   handler.resume();
```

---

[8]https://developers.arcgis.com/javascript/latest/api-reference/esri-
core-watchUtils.html#~PromisedWatchHandle

With this little sample, I may have a custom
component that is updated as the center property
of the view changes. However, I may have some
animation set up for resizing this component or
maybe docking it into a toolbar where it's not
completely visible. The point is that I simply want
to pause the updates for this component so I can
call handler.pause(). Then when the component
is in a state where I want the updates to continue,
I can call handler.resume(). I have found this
pausable() helper to be one of the most useful of
the watchUtils helpers.

I recommend looking through the documentation[9] and just keeping
these helpers in mind when you come across an odd situation while
watching for property changes.

Autocasting

Another powerful feature of using an Accessor is that you can define
properties that can be autocast to a class or module. This allows you to
pass data that *looks like* a certain type and have it converted to that type.

```
1   import Accessor from "esri/core/Accessor";
2   import Extent from "esri/geometry/Extent";
3
4   const Model = Accessor.createSubclass({
5     properties: {
6       extent: Extent
7     }
```

---

[9]https://developers.arcgis.com/javascript/latest/api-reference/esri-
core-watchUtils.html

```
8    });
9
10   export default Model;
```

Now you can pass an extent-like object to this Accessor and have it turned into a real extent.

```
1    const model = new Model({
2      extent: {
3        xmin: -122.68,
4        ymin: 45.53,
5        xmax: -122.45,
6        ymax: 45.6
7      }
8    });
9
10   model.watch("extent", (val) => console.log(val));
```

As you can see, this makes it pretty easy to build up modules and classes that allow you to pass simple data objects that can autocast to more complex objects.

Autocasting becomes so useful in the API that you may even forget that it's there. A great example is when you create a WebMap.

```
1    const webmap = new WebMap({
2      portalItem: {
3        id: "e691172598f04ea8881cd2a4adaa45ba"
4      }
5    });
6
7    const view = new MapView({
8      map: webmap,   //the WebMap instance created above
9      container: "viewDiv"
10   });
```

WebMaps are covered in Chapter 3. But in this case, you are simply passing the id value of a PortalItem to the constructor of a WebMap. Internally, the WebMap knows that the property portalItem is of the type PortalItem. So, by passing an object that has the minimum properties required for a PortalItem, the WebMap can autocast that object to the correct instance.

The ability to simply watch for when a property changes instead of listening for events to occur is something of a new concept if you've been using the 3.*x* version of the API, but I hope you can see the simplicity and flexibility of watching for property changes in the 4.*x* version of the API and gain some real benefits from using this feature.

Extending Accessor

As of version 4.2 of the ArcGIS API for JavaScript, the Accessor documentation now includes the section "Implementing Accessor."[10] The section is pretty extensive, so without regurgitating what it provides, let's look at a couple of basics.

You have already seen how to implement an Accessor on your own using Accessor.createSubclass(). The key here is to provide a properties object that will contain information about your implementation. You have already seen how you can predefine the types of properties.

```
1   const Model = Accessor.createSubclass({
2       properties: {
3         extent: Extent
4       }
5   });
```

---

[10]https://developers.arcgis.com/javascript/latest/guide/implementing-accessor/index.html

But you can take this a step further and have some computed properties.

```
1    const Model = Accessor.createSubclass({
2      properties: {
3        graphic: new Graphic(/* Graphic Properties */),
4        bufferedGeometry: {
5          dependsOn: ["graphic"],
6          get: function() {
7            return geometryEngine.buffer(this.graphic.
             geometry);
8          }
9        }
10     }
11   });
```

In this sample, you want a property for bufferedGeometry, which is based on the graphic value. In this case, I don't want users of my Model to have to use the GeometryEngine on their end, so I can simplify it and provide the value for them.

TypeScript Integration

Version 4.2 of the API also introduced improved TypeScript integration for using Accessors. This improved integration also comes with a set of decorators[11] that simplifies the implementation process.

This means you can update your previous sample to look more like this:

```
1    /// <amd-dependency path="esr/core/tsSupport/
     declareExtendsHelper" name="__exten\
2    ds" />
```

---

[11]https://developers.arcgis.com/javascript/latest/api-reference/esri-core-accessorSupport-decorators.html

```
3   /// <amd-dependency path="esr/core/tsSupport/
    decorateHelper" name="__decorate" />
4
5   import { declared, subclass, property } from
    "esri/core/accessorSupport/decorators";
6
7   @subclass()
8   class Model extends declared(Accessor) {
9
10    @property()
11    graphic: Graphic = new Graphic();
12
13    @property({
14      dependsOn: ["graphic]
15    })
16    get bufferedGeometry(): Geometry {
17      return geometryEngine.buffer(this.graphic.geometry);
18    }
19
20  }
```

The decorators are incredibly useful to make implementing Accessor[12] and defining properties much more explicit. You can review the documentation for decorators for more details.[13]

---

[12]https://developers.arcgis.com/javascript/latest/guide/implementing-accessor/index.html

[13]https://developers.arcgis.com/javascript/latest/api-reference/esri-core-accessorSupport-decorators.html

Collections

Collections[14] in the ArcGIS API 4 for JavaScript API are *array-like* containers of data. They look and act like arrays, but they cannot be iterated over with a `for` loop. Instead, you would use one of the many array methods[15] to work with the collection. Most of these methods are typical array methods[16] that work as expected. Some methods are exclusive to the collection, such as `getItemAt()`.[17]

Without just copying the documentation, I want to point out some methods exclusive to a collection.

- `ofType`:[18] Allows you to create typed collections

- `add`:[19] Works like `Array.prototype.push`[20]

- `addMany`:[21] Takes an array of objects to add to the collection

- `clone`:[22] As advertised, creates a clone of the collection

---

[14]https://developers.arcgis.com/javascript/latest/api-reference/esri-core-Collection.html

[15]https://developers.arcgis.com/javascript/latest/api-reference/esri-core-Collection.html

[16]https://developer.mozilla.org/en-US/docs/Web/JavaScript/Reference/Global_Objects/Array

[17]https://developers.arcgis.com/javascript/latest/api-reference/esri-core-Collection.html#getItemAt

[18]https://developers.arcgis.com/javascript/latest/api-reference/esri-core-Collection.html#.ofType

[19]https://developers.arcgis.com/javascript/latest/api-reference/esri-core-Collection.html#add

[20]https://developer.mozilla.org/en-US/docs/Web/JavaScript/Reference/Global_Objects/Array/push

[21]https://developers.arcgis.com/javascript/latest/api-reference/esri-core-Collection.html#addMany

[22]https://developers.arcgis.com/javascript/latest/api-reference/esri-core-Collection.html#clone

- `remove:`[23] Removes the argument passed in from the collection

- `removeAll:`[24] Empties the collection

- `removeAt:`[25] Easily removes an item from the collection at a specific index

- `removeMany:`[26] Removes all items from the given array

- `reorder:`[27] Moves an item to a new index in the collection

- `toArray:`[28] Exports the collection a normal native array

Another feature of the collection is the ability to listen for change events.

```
1   collection.on("change", ({ added, moved, removed }) =>
    {/*do something cool*/});
```

The change event returns an object with the properties added, moved, and removed. Each property is an array that will contain the items that changed in the collection. This is an incredibly useful feature that you can't get with native JavaScript arrays. You'll be able to watch for any changes done to the collection and act accordingly.

---

[23]https://developers.arcgis.com/javascript/latest/api-reference/esri-core-Collection.html#remove

[24]https://developers.arcgis.com/javascript/latest/api-reference/esri-core-Collection.html#removeAll

[25]https://developers.arcgis.com/javascript/latest/api-reference/esri-core-Collection.html#removeAt

[26]https://developers.arcgis.com/javascript/latest/api-reference/esri-core-Collection.html#removeMany

[27]https://developers.arcgis.com/javascript/latest/api-reference/esri-core-Collection.html#reorder

[28]https://developers.arcgis.com/javascript/latest/api-reference/esri-core-Collection.html#toArray

Promises

One thing that the views and layers all have in common is they are all promises.[29]

Promises are incredibly useful for performing asynchronous operations. You'll find promises throughout the entire API. This is because there are numerous asynchronous operations taking place.

When you create a view, you can check the promise method then to see when the view is done loading and start checking on properties.

```
1   view.then(() => {
2     view.watch("extent.xmin", (xmin) => console.log(xmin));
3   });
```

It's also good practice to start watching for Accessor property changes after the view is loaded and ready. Promises come in handy so you can chain their results.

```
1   view.then(() => {
2     return view.whenLayerView(myLayer);
3   })
4   .then((layerView) => {
5     return watchUtils.whenFalseOnce(layerView, "updating");
6   })
7   .then(({ target: layerView }) => {
8     return layerView.queryFeatures()
9   })
10  .then((features => {
11    view.goTo(features);
12  }))
```

---

[29]https://developer.mozilla.org/en-US/docs/Web/JavaScript/Reference/
Global_Objects/Promise

```
13   .otherwise(error => {
14      // catch errors in the Promise chain here
15   });
```

In this snippet of code, you wait for the view to load, get a LayerView from the view, query the features in the view, and then use the goTo method[30] to animate to the features.

In this sample, you are using the watchUtils module to help check for a property change, but you only care about when the LayerView is done updating so you can get the features. I'll cover this method a little more in the next chapter on Accessors.

The ability to use promises throughout the API is incredibly useful to handle the multiple asynchronous operations that take place in a web mapping application.

Summary

At this point, you should have a pretty good idea of how the core fundamentals of the ArcGIS API for JavaScript work. Having a solid grasp of how Accessors, collections, and promises work will greatly enhance your ability to build applications with the API.

- Accessors provide a way for you to easily watch for property changes, instead of listening for events.

- Collections are useful to store data that may normally sit in an array if you want to know that the collection is updated.

- Promises allow you to work with asynchronous data and, in the case of the views, let you know when they are ready to be used.

---

[30]https://developers.arcgis.com/javascript/latest/api-reference/esri-views-MapView.html#goTo

CHAPTER 5

Scenes

By far one of the most exciting features of ArcGIS API 4 for JavaScript is the introduction of 3D scenes. A 3D scene is a remarkable new way to visualize your data (see Figure 5-1).

Figure 5-1. *Sample scene using Pictometry Imagery*

© Rene Rubalcava 2017
R. Rubalcava, *Introducing ArcGIS API 4 for JavaScript*,
https://doi.org/10.1007/978-1-4842-3282-8_5

You can create and publish scenes using the Scene Viewer,[1] which is part of the ArcGIS Online platform.[2] When you author your scenes in the Scene Viewer, they are saved to your account where you can share them with others. You can then use these scenes with your ArcGIS API 4 for JavaScript application using the item ID of your scene.

Scenes themselves are created and published in ArcGIS Pro.[3] You can update the scene in the Scene Viewer and modify or create new slides.[4] The scenes you can update and modify in the Scene Viewer can then be viewed in your ArcGIS API 4 for JavaScript application.

Loading a WebScene[5] is extremely easy; it's just like loading a WebMap.

```
1    import WebScene from "esri/WebScene";
2    import SceneView from "esri/views/SceneView";
3
4    const scene = new WebScene({
5      portalItem: {
6        id: "082c4fd545104f159db39da11ea1e675"
7      }
8    });
9
10   const view = new SceneView({
11     map: scene,
12     container: "viewDiv"
13   });
```

---

[1]https://www.arcgis.com/home/webscene/viewer.html

[2]https://www.arcgis.com/home/

[3]http://pro.arcgis.com/en/pro-app/help/mapping/map-authoring/author-a-web-scene.htm

[4]https://developers.arcgis.com/javascript/latest/api-reference/esri-webscene-Slide.html

[5]https://developers.arcgis.com/javascript/latest/api-reference/esri-WebScene.html

That's all you have to do to display your scene with the ArcGIS JavaScript API.

What differentiates a scene from a regular map? I'll make this simple: *3D*.

Scenes have elevation data, meaning you can work with terrains and buildings. When you place features on the map, you can drape them, as if you draping a sheet over your bed. You can also billboard the symbols, just like advertising billboards (see Figure 5-2).

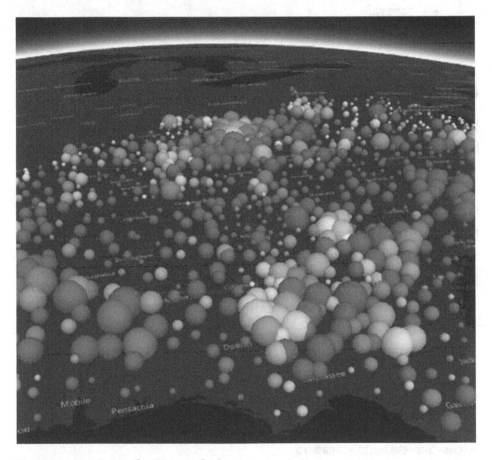

Figure 5-2. *Sample 3D symbols in a scene*

SceneView

The `SceneView` shares a similar API to a `MapView` because they both are based on the `View`[6] module. As you have already learned, views are responsible for the rendering of data in the `Map`, `WebMap`, or `WebScene`.

To understand the `SceneView`, you need to understand a couple of the unique properties you can work with.

- `camera`[7]

- `environment`[8]

camera Property

You can think of the camera as a literal camera positioned at a specific location, pointed in a specific direction, and tilted at a specific angle with a specific field of view. These also happen to be the exact properties[9] of a camera. You can update the camera at any time while your application is running. If you do want to update the camera, you will probably want to use the view's goTo method to animate the view to the new camera settings. If you simply use `view.camera = updatedCamera`, it will not be a smooth transition to the new camera settings.

```
1   const view = new SceneView({
2     map,
3     container: "viewDiv",
```

---

[6]https://developers.arcgis.com/javascript/latest/api-reference/esri-views-View.html

[7]https://developers.arcgis.com/javascript/latest/api-reference/esri-views-SceneView.html#camera

[8]https://developers.arcgis.com/javascript/latest/api-reference/esri-views-SceneView.html#environment

[9]https://developers.arcgis.com/javascript/latest/api-reference/esri-Camera.html#properties

```
4     camera: {
5        position: [7.654, 45.919, 5183],
6        tilt: 80
7     }
8   });
```

9   *At some point in your application, you can update the camera.*

```
10   view.goTo({
11      position: [7.654, 45.919, 7500],
12      tilt: 65
13   });
```

You can view a sample of updating the camera in the demo at https://jsbin.com/sodeda/3.

It should also be noted that the view will not reflect any updates made to the camera directly.

```
1   view.camera.position = updatedPosition; // does not work
```

However, you can clone the camera to keep the current camera settings and update only a single property.

```
1   const camera = view.camera.clone();
2   camera.tilt = 120;
3   view.camera = camera;
4   // or
5   view.goTo(camera);
```

Now I'll show you an interesting sample[10] of how you can clone the camera every time the Scene changes and replay the cameras to create a smooth animation of your view.

---

[10]https://jsbin.com/sodeda/4/edit?js,output

Let's look at some code for this sample:

```
1   <!DOCTYPE html>
2   <html>
3   <head>
4   <meta charset="utf-8">
5   <meta name="viewport" content="initial-scale=1,maximum-
    scale=1,user-scalable=no">
6   <title>4.x 3D Camera Recorder</title>
7   <link rel="stylesheet" href="https://js.arcgis.com/4.5/
    esri/css/main.css">
8   <link rel="stylesheet" href="https://maxcdn.bootstrapcdn.
    com/bootstrap/3.3.5/css/bootstrap.min.css">
9  <link href="https://cdnjs.cloudflare.com/ajax/libs/
   bootstrap-material-design/0.3.0/css/material-fullpalette.
   min.css" rel="stylesheet">
10  </head>
11  <body>
12    <div id="viewDiv"></div>
13    <div id="recorder">
14      <div>
15        <input class="camera-slider" id="slider"
16        type="range" min="1" max="1" step="1" value="1">
17        <a href="javascript:void(0)" id="reverseBtn"
18          title="Play views in reverse"
19          class="btn btn-info btn-fab btn-raised mdi-av-fast-
            rewind"></a>
20        <a href="javascript:void(0)" id="playBtn"
21          title="Play views"
22          class="btn btn-info btn-fab btn-raised mdi-av-play-
            arrow"></a>
```

```
23    <a href="javascript:void(0)" id="stopBtn"
24       title="Pause recording view"
25       class="btn btn-info btn-fab btn-raised mdi-
         av-pause"></a>
26   </div>
27  </div>
28  <script src="https://js.arcgis.com/4.5/"></script>
29 </body>
30 </html>
```

We need to define some styles for our little application

```
1  html, body, #viewDiv {
2     padding: 0;
3     margin: 0;
4     width: 100%;
5     height: 100%;
6  }
7  #recorder {
8     position: absolute;
9     z-index: 999;
10    bottom: 1em;
11    left: 1em;
12    padding: 1em;
13    width: 50%;
14    margin-left: 100px;
15 }
16 #reverse {
17    position: absolute;
18    z-index: 999;
19    bottom: 50px;
20    left: 150px;
21 }
```

```
22   #recorder > input[type=range] {
23     width: 168px;
24   }
25   input[type=range] {
26     -webkit-appearance: none;
27     margin: 18px 0;
28     width: 100%;
29   }
30   input[type=range]:focus {
31     outline: none;
32   }
33   input[type=range]::-webkit-slider-runnable-track {
34     width: 100%;
35     height: 8.4px;
36     cursor: pointer;
37     animate: 0.2s;
38    box-shadow: 1px 1px 1px #000000, 0px 0px 1px #0d0d0d;
39     background: #3071a9;
40     border-radius: 1.3px;
41     border: 0.2px solid #010101;
42   }
43   input[type=range]::-webkit-slider-thumb {
44     box-shadow: 1px 1px 1px #000000, 0px 0px 1px #0d0d0d;
45     border: 1px solid #000000;
46     height: 20px;
47     width: 20px;
48     border-radius: 10px;
49     background: #ffffff;
50     cursor: pointer;
51     -webkit-appearance: none;
52     margin-top: -5px;
53   }
```

```
54  input[type=range]:focus::-webkit-slider-runnable-track {
55    background: #367ebd;
56  }
57  input[type=range]::-moz-range-track {
58    width: 100%;
59    height: 8.4px;
60    cursor: pointer;
61    animate: 0.2s;
62    box-shadow: 1px 1px 1px #000000, 0px 0px 1px #0d0d0d;
63    background: #3071a9;
64    border-radius: 1.3px;
65    border: 0.2px solid #010101;
66  }
67  input[type=range]::-moz-range-thumb {
68    box-shadow: 1px 1px 1px #000000, 0px 0px 1px #0d0d0d;
69    border: 1px solid #000000;
70    height: 20px;
71    width: 20px;
72    border-radius: 10px;
73    background: #ffffff;
74    cursor: pointer;
75  }
76  input[type=range]::-ms-track {
77    width: 100%;
78    height: 8.4px;
79    cursor: pointer;
80    animate: 0.2s;
81    background: transparent;
82    border-color: transparent;
83    border-width: 16px 0;
84    color: transparent;
85  }
```

```
 86   input[type=range]::-ms-fill-lower {
 87     background: #2a6495;
 88     border: 0.2px solid #010101;
 89     border-radius: 2.6px;
 90     box-shadow: 1px 1px 1px #000000, 0px 0px 1px #0d0d0d;
 91   }
 92   input[type=range]::-ms-fill-upper {
 93     background: #3071a9;
 94     border: 0.2px solid #010101;
 95     border-radius: 2.6px;
 96     box-shadow: 1px 1px 1px #000000, 0px 0px 1px #0d0d0d;
 97   }
 98   input[type=range]::-ms-thumb {
 99     box-shadow: 1px 1px 1px #000000, 0px 0px 1px #0d0d0d;
100     border: 1px solid #000000;
101     height: 20px;
102     width: 20px;
103     border-radius: 10px;
104     background: #ffffff;
105     cursor: pointer;
106   }
107   input[type=range]:focus::-ms-fill-lower {
108     background: #3071a9;
109   }
110   input[type=range]:focus::-ms-fill-upper {
111     background: #367ebd;
112   }
```

Now we can write up the code for our sample application.

```
1     require([
2     'esri/Map',
3     'esri/views/SceneView',
```

```
4     'esri/core/watchUtils',
5     'esri/core/Scheduler',
6     'dojo/on'
7  ], function(Map, SceneView, watchUtils, Scheduler, on) {
8     class CameraRecorder {
9     constructor(params) {
10      this.view = params.view;
11      this.cameras = [ null ];
12      this.timer = null;
13      this.watcher = null;
14      this.handler = null;
15      this.intervalID = null;
16      this.isPlaying = false;
17    this.slider = document.getElementById('slider');
18    this.reverseBtn = document.getElementById('reverseBtn');
19    this.reverseBtn.addEventListener('click', this.
      playReverse.bind(this));
20    this.playBtn = document.getElementById('playBtn');
21    this.playBtn.addEventListener('click', this.play.
      bind(this));
22    this.stopBtn = document.getElementById('stopBtn');
23    this.stopBtn.addEventListener('click', this.stop.
      bind(this));
24    }
25    clear() {
26      if (this.watcher) {
27        this.watcher.remove();
28      }
29      if (this.handler) {
30        this.handler.remove();
31      }
```

```
32      if (this.timer) {
33        this.timer.remove();
34      }
35      this.recordStart();
36    }
37    recordStart() {
38      if (this.isPlaying || this.isPaused) {
39        return;
40      }
41      this.timer = Scheduler.schedule(() => {
42        this._cameraWatch();
43        this._sliderWatch();
44      });
45    }
46    play() {
47      if (this.isPlaying) {
48        return;
49      }
50      this.playBtn.classList.toggle('btn-info');
51      this.playBtn.classList.toggle('btn-success');
52      this._play(false);
53    }
54    stop() {
55      this.isPaused = !this.isPaused;
56      this.stopBtn.classList.toggle('btn-info');
57      this.stopBtn.classList.toggle('btn-danger');
58      if (!this.isPaused) {
59        this.recordStart();
60      }
61    }
```

```
62    playReverse() {
63      if (this.isPlaying) {
64        return;
61      }
62      this.reverseBtn.classList.toggle('btn-info');
63      this.reverseBtn.classList.toggle('btn-success');
64      this._play(true);
65    }
66    _cameraWatch() {
67      const view = this.view;
68      const cameras = this.cameras;
69      const slider = this.slider;
70      this.watcher = view.watch('camera', (val) => {
71        cameras.push(val.clone());
72        slider.max = slider.value = cameras.length;
73        this.clear();
74      });
75    }
76    _sliderWatch() {
77      const view = this.view;
78      const cameras = this.cameras;
79      this.handler = on(this.slider, 'input', (e) => {
80        const val =Number(e.target.value);
81        view.goTo(cameras[val] || view.camera.clone());
82        this.clear();
83      });
84    }
85    _play(inReverse) {
86      this.isPlaying = true;
87      let intervalID = this.intervalID;
88      const slider = this.slider;
89      const view = this.view;
```

```
90          const cameras = this.cameras;
91          let len = cameras.length;
92          let i = 0;
93          intervalID = setInterval(() => {
94            if (!inReverse) {
95              slider.value = i;
96              view.goTo(cameras[i++] || view.camera.clone());
97              if (i === len) {
98                clearInterval(intervalID);
99                this.playBtn.classList.toggle('btn-info');
100               this.playBtn.classList.toggle('btn-success');
101               this.isPlaying = false;
102               this.recordStart();
103             }
104           }
105           else {
106             slider.value = len;
107             view.camera = cameras[len--] || view.camera.clone();
108             if (len < 1) {
109               clearInterval(intervalID);
110               this.reverseBtn.classList.toggle('btn-info');
111               this.reverseBtn.classList.toggle('btn-success');
112               this.isPlaying = false;
113               this.recordStart();
114             }
115           }
116         }, 15);
117     }
118   }
119   const map = new Map({
120     basemap: 'streets'
121   });
```

```
122  const view = new SceneView({
123    container: 'viewDiv',
124    map: map,
125    scale: 240000000
126  });
127  const camRecorder = new CameraRecorder({ view });
128  view.then(() => camRecorder.recordStart());
129  });
```

CameraRecorder class creates a CameraRecorder widget. This class will watch for the camera property of the SceneView to change, and when it does, it will clone the camera and save the cloned cameras into an array for later use. It has buttons to replay the cameras, replay them in reverse, or pause the watchers from saving the camera changes. It also provides a slider so that you can play back to a certain Camera point again. This small application shows the usefulness of having access to a Camera in the SceneView so that not only can you save a snapshot of the SceneView but also manipulate the Camera as needed.

environment Property

What does the environment property do? Notice all the really cool shadows cast by the buildings and objects in a 3D scene? That is controlled via the environment property. More specifically, it is handled via the lighting[11] property of the environment.

Essentially, this allows you to control the position of the sun in your scene. Not only that, but you can define it by the date and time of day. Did you know that the locations of the stars in a scene are accurate to the date? That's a pretty powerful detail.

---

[11]https://developers.arcgis.com/javascript/latest/api-reference/esri-webscene-Lighting.html

Most of the `lighting` properties are fairly straightforward; `date` and `displayUTCOffset` are pretty self-explanatory. The `directShadowsEnabled` property just turns the shadows on or off. The one that may throw you for a loop is `ambientOcclusionEnabled`.[12] This is basically how light is reflected off surfaces. The `ambientOcclusionEnabled` property is disabled on lower-powered devices, such as mobile phones for performance purposes (see Figure 5-3).

Figure 5-3. *Updated environment settings in a scene*

---

[12]https://developers.arcgis.com/javascript/latest/api-reference/esri-webscene-Lighting.html#ambientOcclusionEnabled

Local Scenes

Local scenes are an extremely useful tool for 3D visualizations. A local scene will allow you to view subsurface data in a 3D environment. You need two things when you want to create a local scene. You need to set the SceneView#viewingMode property and provide a SceneView#clippingArea property.

```
1   const view = new SceneView({
2       container: "viewDiv",
3       map: map,
4       viewingMode: "local",
5       clippingArea: myClippingArea
6   });
```

A local scene allows you to flatten a 3D surface and clip it to a particular extent so you can view subsurface elements. This is currently useful to view wells, earthquake data, fracking data, and essentially any data that can be mapped underground. There isn't really a straightforward method to display pipeline data at the moment.

Here is a sample of how you might create a local scene to view some wells in a specific area. You can see a live demo here:[13]

```
1   require([
2     "esri/Map",
3     "esri/views/SceneView",
4     "esri/layers/FeatureLayer",
5     "esri/widgets/Home"
6   ], function(Map, SceneView, FeatureLayer, Home
7   ) {
8
```

---

[13]http://jsbin.com/boqehodozu/4/edit?js,output

```
9      const wellsUrl = "http://services.arcgis.com/
       jDGuO8tYggdCCnUJ/arcgis/rest/serv\
10   ices/CA%20Class%20II%20Injection%20Wells/FeatureServer/6";
11
12     const wellsSurfaceRenderer = {
13     type: "simple",
14     symbol: {
15       type: "point-3d",
16       symbolLayers: [{
17         type: "icon",
18         material: {
19           color: "#0D2644"
20         },
21         resource: {
22           primitive: "circle"
23         },
24         size: 4
25       }]
26     }
27   };
28
29     const wellsDepthRenderer = {
30      type: "simple",
31      symbol: {
32        type: "point-3d",
33        symbolLayers: [{
34          type: "object",
35          resource: {
36            primitive: "cylinder"
37          },
```

```
38        width: 50
39      }]
40    },
41    visualVariables: [
42    {
43      type: "size",
44      field: "WellDepthA",
45      axis: "height",
46      stops: [
47      {
48        value: 1,
49        size: -0.3048 // meters!
50      },
51      {
52        value: 10000,
53        size: -3048 // meters!
54      }]
55    },
56    {
57      type: "size",
58      axis: "width",
59      useSymbolValue: true // sets the width to 50m
60    },
61    {
62      type: "color",
63      field: "WellDepthA",
64      stops: [
65        {
66          value: 0,
67          color: "#FFFCD4",
68        },
```

```
69              {
70                value: 10000,
71                color: "#FF0000"
72              }
73          ]
74        }
75        ]
76    });
77
78      // Underground wells
79      const wellsLyr = new FeatureLayer({
80        url: wellsUrl,
81        definitionExpression: "WellDepthA > 0",
82        outFields: ["*"],
83        popupTemplate: {
84          title: "Well",
85          content: "{*}"
86        },
87        renderer: wellsDepthRenderer,
88        // Keep the cylinders from poking above the ground
89        elevationInfo: {
90          mode: "relative-to-ground",
91          offset: -10
92        }
93    });
94
95      // Wells shown on surface
96      const wellsSurfaceLyr = new FeatureLayer({
97        url: wellsUrl,
98        definitionExpression: "WellDepthA > 0",
99        outFields: ["*"],
```

```
100      popupTemplate: {
101        title: "Well",
102        content: "{*}"
103      },
104      renderer: wellsSurfaceRenderer,
105      elevationInfo: {
106        mode: "on-the-ground"
107      }
108    });
109
110    const losAngelesExtent = {
111      xmax: -13151509,
112      xmin: -13160242,
113      ymax: 3999804,
114      ymin: 3992447,
115      spatialReference: {
116        wkid: 102100
117      }
118    };
119
120    const map = new Map({
121      basemap: "topo",
122      layers: [
123        wellsLyr,
124        wellsSurfaceLyr
125      ]
126    });
127
128    const view = new SceneView({
129      container: "viewDiv",
130      map: map,
```

```
131        viewingMode: "local",
132        clippingArea: losAngelesExtent,
133        extent: losAngelesExtent,
134        constraints: {
135          collision: {
136            enabled: false
137          },
138          tilt: {
139            max: 360
140          }
141        },
142        environment: {
143          atmosphere: null,
144          starsEnabled: false
145        }
146      });
147
148      const homeBtn = new Home({
149        view: view
150      }, "homeDiv");
151      homeBtn.startup();
152    });
```

You should get an application that looks similar to Figure 5-4.

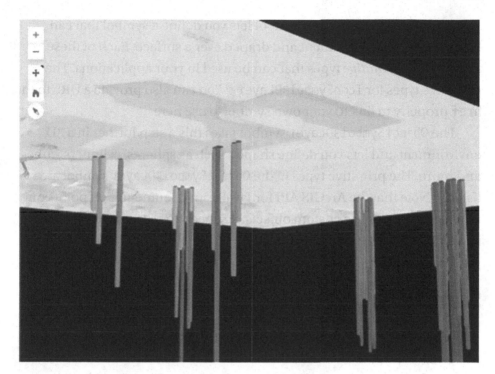

Figure 5-4. *Local scene demo*

We are taking advantage of lots of autocasting in this example, but let's take a look at some of the modules being used that are specific to 3D. You are being introduced to a few new symbols in this demo: `PointSymbol3D`,[14] `IconSymbol3DLayer`,[15] and `ObjectSymbol3DLayer`.[16]

The `PointSymbol3D` symbol does exactly what it says it does. It allows you to display point data in a 3D `SceneView`. Alone, it doesn't do much, but that's what the other two symbols are used for.

---

[14]https://developers.arcgis.com/javascript/latest/api-reference/esri-symbols-PointSymbol3D.html

[15]https://developers.arcgis.com/javascript/latest/api-reference/esri-symbols-IconSymbol3DLayer.html

[16]https://developers.arcgis.com/javascript/latest/api-reference/esri-symbols-ObjectSymbol3DLayer.html

The IconSymbol3DLayer symbol lets you define a symbol that can be used in a 3D environment and draped over a surface. Each of these symbols has *primitive* types that can be used in your applications. The primitive types for IconSymbol3DLayer.[17] You can also provide a URL to the href property to link to your own symbol to use here.

The ObjectSymbol3DLayer symbol takes this a step further in a 3D environment and lets you define shapes, such as spheres, cylinders, cubes, and more. The primitive types of the ObjectSymbol3DLayer symbol are listed.[18] Note that the ArcGIS API for JavaScript documentation points out that if you want to use custom objects, you need to create and export them in ArcGIS Pro via the tutorial.[19]

Summary

This chapter covered the basics of working with scenes in the ArcGIS API for JavaScript. 3D visualizations are the newest and one of the more exciting features in the ArcGIS API 4 for JavaScript. They provide an opportunity for users to explore their data in entirely new ways, and their usefulness will only grow in future releases. You should now be familiar with the following:

- Creating a SceneView and using WebScenes

- Working with the camera in a scene

---

[17]https://developers.arcgis.com/javascript/latest/api-reference/
esri-symbols-IconSymbol3DLayer.html#resource

[18]https://developers.arcgis.com/javascript/latest/api-reference/
esri-symbols-ObjectSymbol3DLayer.html#resource

[19]https://github.com/Esri/arcgis-pro-sdk-community-samples/tree/
master/Map-Authoring/ExportWeb3DObjectResource#exportweb3dobje
ctresource

- Customizing the environment for a scene in your application

- Creating local scenes for focused visualizations and viewing subsurface features

CHAPTER 6

Popup

Since version 1.0 of the ArcGIS API for JavaScript, a user's first interaction when clicking a map has usually been to get a popup. The Popup[1] widget is typically the first entry point to the raw data behind the visualizations displayed on the map. A well-defined visualization of data on a map may tell you the population density of a city compared to an adjacent city based on a color from a color ramp or the size of the point displayed. But your first look at those raw numbers is probably going to come from clicking that feature and viewing the data in the popup.

Because popups are so key to exploring the data in your map, there are various options for configuring how that data is displayed.

Fields and Aliases

You can get started quickly with defining a popupTemplate for popups on a layer like so:

```
1   const featureLayer = new FeatureLayer({
2     url: "https://sampleserver6.arcgisonline.com/arcgis/rest/
      services/Census/MapSe\
```

---

[1]https://developers.arcgis.com/javascript/latest/api-reference/esri-widgets-Popup.html

© Rene Rubalcava 2017
R. Rubalcava, *Introducing ArcGIS API 4 for JavaScript*,
https://doi.org/10.1007/978-1-4842-3282-8_6

```
3    rver/3",
4      outFields: ["*"],
5      popupTemplate: {
6        title: "Name: {STATE_NAME}",
7        content: "{*}"
8      }
9    });
```

This will create a popup with the title "Name: Foghorn Leghorn" if the NAME field for that feature is Foghorn Leghorn. By defining the content as "{*}", the popup will display a simple table showing all the field names and their values.

That is just about as simple of a Popup widget as you can define. But you can take this a step further.

Probably the easiest way to work with popups for your layers and maps is to configure the Popup[2] in the ArcGIS Online map viewer. The configurations you make to your popup will be reflected in your application if you load it via a WebMap or via a PortalItem, as we discussed in previous chapters.

You can configure the Popup to display an alias instead of the actual field name if you want. You configure this in the content property of the popupTemplate.

```
1    const featureLayer = new FeatureLayer({
2      url: "https://sampleserver6.arcgisonline.com/arcgis/
         rest/services/Census/MapSe\
```

---

[2]https://doc.arcgis.com/en/arcgis-online/create-maps/configure-pop-ups.htm

```
 3   rver/3",
 4       outFields: ["*"],
 5     popupTemplate: {
 6         title: "Name: {STATE_NAME}",
 7       content: [
 8          {
 9             type: "fields",
10             fieldInfos: [
11               {
12                  fieldName: "POP2000",
13                  visible: true,
14                  label: "Population for year 2000",
15                  format: {
16                    places: 0,
17                    digitSeparator: true
18                  }
19               },
20               {
21                  fieldName: "POP2007",
22                  visible: true,
23                  label: "Population for year 2007",
24                  format: {
25                    places: 0,
26                    digitSeparator: true
27                  }
28               }
29             ]
30          }
31        ]
32      }
33   });
```

The previous sample will display two fields, the POP2000 and POP2007 fields. However, you can provide a label property for each field that is different from the actual field name. Since you are dealing with fields that have numeric values, you can also define how those numeric values are displayed. In this case, you want zero decimal places and no separator for digits, which varies based on the locale.

If your data had a date field, you could also define a date format.

```
1  {
2    fieldName: "FAKEDATE",
3    visible: true,
4    label: "Fake Date Field",
5    format: {
6      dateFormat: "short-date"
7    }
8  }
```

That's pretty simple, right?

You could even use plain HTML in the content if you wanted to really customize the output.

```
1  const featureLayer = new FeatureLayer({
2    url: "https://sampleserver6.arcgisonline.com/arcgis/
       rest/services/Census/MapSe\
3  rver/2",
4    outFields: ["*"],
5    popupTemplate: {
6      title: "Name: {STATE_NAME}",
7      content: `
8        <section>
9          <h4>{STATE_ABBR}</h4>
10         <hr />
11         <ul>
```

```
12          <li>Year 2000 Pop: {POP2000}</li>
13          <li>Year 2007 Pop: {POP2007}</li>
14          <li>Total Households: {HOUSEHOLDS}</li>
15        </ul>
16      </section>
17              `
18    }
19  });
```

You could even use a function for the content to process it a bit further. Let's assume you had a known geometry in your application, perhaps some sort of fenced-off area. You want to notify the user when they click an item that the location is within this fenced-off area.

```
1   const featureLayer = new FeatureLayer({
2     url: URL,
3     outFields: ["*"],
4     popupTemplate: {
5       title: "Name: {name}",
6       content({ graphic }) {
7         const isWithin = geometryEngine.
           contains(fencedGeometry, graphic.geometry);
8         return `
9           Location ${isWithin ? "is" : "is not"} currently
             within fenced area.
10          `;
11       }
12     }
13  });
```

This is just another way you can customize the content of your popup.

You can take this a step further and query multiple layers based on a click of the view.

```
1    view.on("click", ({ mapPoint }) => {
2      const screenPoint = view.toScreen(mapPoint);
3      view.hitTest(screenPoint).then(({ results }) => {
4        if (results[0].graphic) {
5          view.popup.open({
6            location: mapPoint,
7            promises: [() => {
8              query.geometry = results[0].graphic.geometry;
9              return qTask.execute(query).then(({ features })
                 => {
10               var names = features.map((feature) => {
11                 return feature.attributes.state_name;
12               }).join(", ");
13               return "{route} crosses the following States:
                   " + names;
14             });
15           }]
16         });
17       }
18     });
19   });
```

This particular sample will query a service to see whether a graphic intersects features from that service. When the queries added to the promises property in the argument for the popup are complete, the popup will open and display your custom results.

You can even use Arcade[3] expressions in your popup.

```
1   const featureLayer = new FeatureLayer({
2     url: "https://sampleserver6.arcgisonline.com/arcgis/
      rest/services/Census/MapSe\
3   rver/2",
4     outFields: ["*"],
5     popupTemplate: {
6       title: "Name: {STATE_NAME}",
7       expressionInfos: [
8         {
9           name: "percent-change",
10          title: "% change from 2000 to 2007",
11          expression: "Abs((($feature.POP2000 - $feature.
            POP2007) / $feature.POP20\
12  00) * 100) + '%'"
13        }
14      ],
15      content: "The percent change from 2000 to 2007 was
        {expression/percent-chang\
16  e}"
17    }
18  });
```

As you can see, it's not difficult to customize how the popup will display the data.

---

[3]https://developers.arcgis.com/arcade/

MediaInfos

The content of the popup can also consist of charts based on the data of the feature. You can define this in a similar fashion as configuring the fieldInfos for the PopupTemplate.

```
1   {
2     type: "media",
3     mediaInfos: [
4       {
5         title: "<b>Population</b>",
6         type: "column-chart",
7         caption: "",
8         value: {
9           theme: "BlueDusk",
10          fields: [ "POP2000", "POP2007" ]
11        }
12      }
13    ]
14  }
```

What this is going to do is display a column-chart for the population data provided in the fields POP2000 and POP2007. Your other choices for the type of media are image, pie-chart, bar-chart, or line-chart. If the type is image, you would provide a sourceURL property instead of a fields property. The themes you can use are based on the Dojox charting library themes.[4] You can read more about the mediaInfos options in the documentation.[5]

---

[4]https://download.dojotoolkit.org/release-1.10.0/dojo-release-1.10.0/dojox/charting/tests/theme_preview.html

[5]https://developers.arcgis.com/javascript/latest/api-reference/esri-PopupTemplate.html#media

Custom Actions

One of the most interesting additions to the ArcGIS API 4 for JavaScript is the ability to add custom actions. Custom actions let you add small buttons to a popup that can be used for various tasks. You can use it to open new web pages, perform queries, or perform other tasks.

In this sample, you are going to perform a search based on the city name for beer-related events in that city.

```
1    require([
2      "esri/views/MapView",
3      "esri/Map",
4      "esri/layers/Layer"
5    ], function(
6            MapView, Map, Layer
7            ) {
8
9      const map = new Map({
10       basemap: "streets-navigation-vector"
11     });
12
13     const view = new MapView({
14       map: map,
15       container: "viewDiv",
16       center: [-117.24, 34.05],
17       zoom: 8
18     });
19
20     view.popup.on("trigger-action", ({ action }) => {
21       if (action.id === "alcohol-details") {
22         var attributes = view.popup.viewModel.
             selectedFeature.attributes;
```

```
23          var name = attributes.NAME;
24          window.open(`https://www.google.com/search?q=${name}
            Beer events`);
25        }
26    });
27
28    Layer.fromPortalItem({
29      portalItem: {
30        id: "c531f67a12254c27af9479d436e23850"
31      }
32    })
33    .then((layer) => {
34      layer.popupTemplate = {
35        title: '{Name}',
36        content: '{*}',
37        actions: [{
38            id: 'alcohol-details',
39            className: 'esri-icon-description',
40            title: 'Events'
41        }]
42      };
43      map.add(layer);
44    })
45    .otherwise(err => console.log(err));
46  });
```

You can find a demo of this application at http://jsbin.com/
namufut/2/edit?js,output.

The main thing to remember is that when you define the
PopupTemplate, you want to define an actions property that contains an
array of the various custom actions you may want to use.

```
1  {
2    title: '{Name}',
3    content: '{*}',
4    actions: [{
5        id: 'alcohol-details',
6        className: 'esri-icon-description',
7        title: 'Events'
8    }]
9  }
```

The className property is used to define a custom icon. This can be an icon you define in your CSS code or one of the icons provided in the API.[6] You could also provide an image property that is the URL of an image you want to use. If you don't define a className or image, there is a default icon that will be provided. You can read more about custom actions in the documentation.[7]

The custom actions can also come in handy if you want to make requests to third-party web services such as a custom API that is used to provide detailed information about customers.

```
1  view.popup.on("trigger-action", ({ action }) => {
2    if (action.id === "customer-details") {
3      var attributes = view.popup.viewModel.selectedFeature.
         attributes;
4      var customerGroup = attributes.CUSTOMER_GROUP;
5      esriRequest(customAPIURL, {
6        query: {
7          group: customerGroup
```

---

[6]https://developers.arcgis.com/javascript/latest/guide/esri-icon-font/
index.html

[7]https://developers.arcgis.com/javascript/latest/api-reference/esri-
PopupTemplate.html#actions

```
 8              },
 9              responseType: "json"
10          })
11          .then({ data } => {
12              // parse data and update popup content
13          })
14          .otherwise(error => console.log(error));
15      }
16  });
```

Summary

In this chapter, you learned how to define a `PopupTemplate`.[8] You also learned how to set up the fields and field aliases you can use in your `PopupTemplate`, giving you more fine-grained control over how your data is displayed. The `PopupTemplate` can even contain custom HTML or media elements such as charts to provide a deeper understanding of the data. You also saw how you can use custom actions in the `PopupTemplate` to perform some custom tasks such as searching the Web or accessing third-party web services to add even more value to your data.

The `Popup` is typically the first entry point users have to details of the data on the map. It is widely used and has a lot of capabilities. Anyone developing with the ArcGIS API for JavaScript would do well to learn how to use it to its full capabilities.

In the next chapter, you will look at how you can use the new widget framework in the ArcGIS API for JavaScript to create a custom widget!

---

[8]https://developers.arcgis.com/javascript/latest/api-reference/esri-PopupTemplate.html

CHAPTER 7

Widgets

Version 4 of the ArcGIS API for JavaScript introduced its own widget framework[1] to build custom widgets. The custom widget development is powered by a virtual DOM[2] library called MaquetteJS.[3] This replaces the older Dojo Dijit[4] framework that was previously used to build widgets. Although Dijit is a perfectly stable and battle-tested widget framework, a virtual DOM library allows you to work with an abstract version of the DOM, making it efficient to find changes and update the DOM.

Prerequisites

Custom widget development, however, does have one prerequisite you should be aware of: TypeScript.[5] Much of the tooling used for custom widget development, such as the Accessor decorators discussed in earlier chapters, require the use of TypeScript.

---

[1] https://developers.arcgis.com/javascript/latest/guide/custom-widget/index.html

[2] https://medium.com/cardlife-app/what-is-virtual-dom-c0ec6d6a925c#.j4jqazh5j

[3] http://maquettejs.org/

[4] https://dojotoolkit.org/reference-guide/1.10/dijit/

[5] www.typescriptlang.org/

I highly recommend you review the TypeScript tutorials.[6] I also highly recommend the following courses on Egghead.io:[7]

- Up and Running with TypeScript[8]
- Using Types Effectively in TypeScript[9]

Typings

You can read more about installing the ArcGIS API or JavaScript typings on GitHub.[10] The key here is that you can easily install the typings using `npm install --save @types/arcgis-js-api`.

It should be noted that this does not install the Dojo typings. If you wanted to use some Dojo modules in your TypeScript development, you can get dojo-typings[11] and set them up in a `tsconfig.json` file like this:

```
1     "types": [ "arcgis-js-api" ],
2     "include": [
3       "./src/app/**/*"
4     ],
5     "exclude": [
6       "node_modules"
7     ],
8     "files": [
9       "node_modules/dojo-typings/dojo/1.11/modules.d.ts",
10      "node_modules/dojo-typings/dijit/1.11/modules.d.ts",
11      "node_modules/dojo-typings/dojox/1.11/modules.d.ts",
```

---

[6]www.typescriptlang.org/docs/tutorial.html
[7]https://egghead.io
[8]https://egghead.io/courses/up-and-running-with-typescript
[9]https://egghead.io/courses/use-types-effectively-in-typescript
[10]https://github.com/Esri/jsapi-resources/tree/master/4.x/typescript
[11]https://github.com/dojo/typings

```
12        "node_modules/dojo-typings/custom/dgrid/1.1/
          dgrid.d.ts",
13        "node_modules/dojo-typings/custom/dstore/1.1/
          dstore.d.ts",
14        "node_modules/intern/typings/intern/intern.d.ts"
15    ]
```

You can read more about the `tsconfig.json` file.[12] The `tsconfig.json` file is used to configure the TypeScript compiler.

JSX

This updated widget framework also introduces the use of JSX,[13] which was popularized by React.[14] JSX looks very much like HTML in JavaScript, except the syntax needs a compilation step to turn the JSX into JavaScript functions.

For example, the JSX `<h1>hello!</h1>` would be compiled to a function that looks like `h('h1', 'hello!')`. This method of creating DOM elements is called HyperScript.[15] In the case of using JSX in custom widget development with the ArcGIS API for JavaScript, you don't need to concern yourself with HyperScript.

Building a Custom Widget

Before diving right into building a custom widget, you can find the source code for the demo application on GitHub (see Figure 7-1).[16]

---

[12]https://www.typescriptlang.org/docs/handbook/tsconfig-json.html
[13]https://facebook.github.io/react/docs/introducing-jsx.html
[14]https://facebook.github.io/react/
[15]https://github.com/dominictarr/hyperscript
[16]https://github.com/odoe/esrijs4-ts-demo

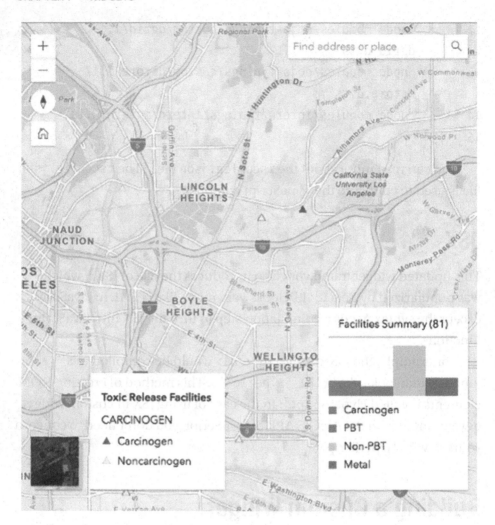

Figure 7-1. *Custom widget development*

The widget you will build in this example is going to display a chart representing the data visible in the map view. The key is to make sure the chart is based only on visible data so that it will update as you pan around the map.

Store and ViewModel

The first step is to build an application store. This application store will contain properties to describe the state of your application. In this application, you are concerned about the View and the WebMap. You can refer to the early chapters for information on how to use the Accessor module[17] for a task like this.

For each TypeScript file that extends Accessor, you will want to add the following amd-dependency lines:

```
1    /// <amd-dependency path="esri/core/tsSupport/
     declareExtendsHelper" name="__exte\
2    nds" />
3    /// <amd-dependency path="esri/core/tsSupport/
     decorateHelper" name="__decorate" \
4    />
```

I'll omit them from the following samples, but be aware that they are required.

```
1    // app/stores/app.ts
2    import EsriMap = require("esri/Map");
3    import MapView = require("esri/views/MapView");
4    import Accessor = require("esri/core/Accessor");
5
6    import {
7      subclass,
8      declared,
9      property
10     } from "esri/core/accessorSupport/decorators";
11
```

---

[17]https://developers.arcgis.com/javascript/latest/guide/implementing-accessor/index.html

113

```
12   type UIParams = {
13     element: any,
14     position?: string
15   };
16
17   interface Store {
18     webmap: EsriMap;
19     view: MapView;
20
21     addToUI(params: UIParams): void;
22   }
23
24   @subclass("app.stores.AppStore")
25   class AppStore extends declared(Accessor) implements Store
   {
26
27     @property()
28     webmap: EsriMap;
29
30     @property()
31     view: MapView;
32
33     addToUI({ element, position }: UIParams) {
34       this.view.ui.add(element, position);
35     }
36
37   }
38
39   export default new AppStore();
```

You have two properties on the store that are watchable, webmap and view. You also add a method, addToUI(), that acts as a proxy to add components to the UI for you. Also, notice how you export the module: export default new AppStore();. This will create a singleton of your store so a new store is not created every time a module imports it.

The next thing you are going to do is build a ViewModel for your custom widget. The ViewModel behaves very much like the application store. It will be the job of the ViewModel to watch for changes to the application store and update its own state based on those changes. It is also the job of the ViewModel to manage the business logic of the widget by performing any queries or operations on data based on the application store.

```
1    // app/widgets/viewmodels/summaryviewmodel.ts
2
3    import Accessor = require("esri/core/Accessor");
4    import watchUtils = require("esri/core/watchUtils");
5
6    import FeatureLayerView = require("esri/views/layers/
     FeatureLayerView");
7    import Graphic = require("esri/Graphic");
8
9    import Query = require("esri/tasks/support/Query");
10
11   import {
12     subclass,
13     declared,
14     property
15     } from "esri/core/accessorSupport/decorators";
16
17   import store from "../../stores/app";
18
```

```
19    const { init, whenOnce, whenFalse } = watchUtils;

20

21    export type Stats = {

22      "Carcinogen": number,

23      "PBT": number,

24      "Non-PBT": number,

25      "Metal": number

26    };

27

28    const stats: Stats = {

29      "Carcinogen": 0, // CARCINOGEN == "Yes"

30      "PBT": 0,        // CLASS == "PBT"

31      "Non-PBT": 0,    // CLASS == "Non-PBT"

32      "Metal": 0       // METAL == "Yes"

33    };

34

35    function errorHandler (error: Error) {

36      console.log("LayerView Query Error", error);

37    }

38

39    @subclass("app.widgets.viewmodels.summaryviewmodel")

40    class SummaryViewModel extends declared(Accessor) {

41

42      @property()

43      count: number = 0;

44

45      @property()

46      stats: Stats = stats;

47

48      constructor() {

49        super();
```

```
50      whenOnce(store, "view").then(_ => {
51        return store.webmap.findLayerById("tri");
52      })
53      .then(layer => {
54        return store.view.whenLayerView(layer);
55      })
56      .then(this.watchLayerView.bind(this))
57      .otherwise(errorHandler);
58    }
59
60    private watchLayerView (layerView: FeatureLayerView) {
61      const queryFeatures = this.queryLayerView(layerView);
62      init(store, "view.stationary", _ => {
63        if (layerView.updating) {
64          whenFalse(layerView, "updating", queryFeatures.
            bind(this));
65        }
66        else {
67          queryFeatures();
68        }
69      });
70    }
71
72    private queryLayerView(layerView: FeatureLayerView) {
73      return () => layerView.queryFeatures(
74        new Query({
75          geometry: store.view.extent
76        })).then(this.parseResults.bind(this)
77      );
78    }
79
```

```
80      private parseResults(results: Graphic[]) {
81        const _stats = (<any> Object).assign({}, stats);
82        results.forEach(({ attributes: attr }) => {
83          if (attr.CARCINOGEN === "Yes") {
84            _stats["Carcinogen"]++;
85          }
86          if (attr.CLASS === "PBT") {
87            _stats["PBT"]++;
88          }
89          else if (attr.CLASS === "Non-PBT") {
90            _stats["Non-PBT"]++;
91          }
92          if (attr.METAL === "Yes") {
93            _stats["Metal"]++;
94          }
95        });
96        this.set({
97          count: results.length,
98          stats: _stats
99        });
100      }
101
102    }
103
104    export default SummaryViewModel;
```

After importing all the dependencies for your ViewModel, you are going to create a type that you can use for the data used in your chart. This type is going to hold counts for values in your FeatureLayer.

```
1    export type Stats = {
2      "Carcinogen": number,
3      "PBT": number,
```

```
4     "Non-PBT": number,
5     "Metal": number
6   };
```

These are the four values you are going to display in your chart. Then you create a data object based on that type with initial values of 0.

```
1   const stats: Stats = {
2     "Carcinogen": 0, // CARCINOGEN == "Yes"
3     "PBT": 0,        // CLASS == "PBT"
4     "Non-PBT": 0,    // CLASS == "Non-PBT"
5     "Metal": 0       // METAL == "Yes"
6   };
```

You can see some notes here to let you know what the string values in the data equate to for each category. You have two watchable properties on the ViewMode, count and stats.

When you initialize the ViewModel, you are going to listen for when the view is updated and then find the FeatureLayerView[18] you are interested in for your charts.

```
1     ...
2     constructor() {
3       super();
4       whenOnce(store, "view").then(_ => {
5         return store.webmap.findLayerById("tri");
6       })
7       .then(layer => {
8         return store.view.whenLayerView(layer);
9       })
```

---

[18]https://developers.arcgis.com/javascript/latest/api-reference/esri-views-layers-FeatureLayerView.html

119

```
10        .then(this.watchLayerView.bind(this))
11        .otherwise(errorHandler);
12    }
13    ...
```

The next thing you will do is to watch for when view.stationary changes to query the FeatureLayerView for data using the extent of the view to limit your results to visible data.

```
1     ...
2     private watchLayerView(layerView: FeatureLayerView) {
3       const queryFeatures = this.queryLayerView(layerView);
4       init(store, "view.stationary", _ => {
5         if (layerView.updating) {
6           whenFalse(layerView, "updating", queryFeatures.
              bind(this));
7         }
8         else {
9           queryFeatures();
10        }
11      });
12    }
13
14    private queryLayerView(layerView: FeatureLayerView) {
15      return () => layerView.queryFeatures(
16        new Query({
17            geometry: store.view.extent
18          })).then(this.parseResults.bind(this)
19        );
20    }
21    ...
```

When the visible data is found, you need to convert the results to match the data object used for your charts.

```
1    private parseResults(results: Graphic[]) {
2      const _stats = (<any> Object).assign({}, stats);
3      results.forEach(({ attributes: attr }) => {
4        if (attr.CARCINOGEN === "Yes") {
5          _stats["Carcinogen"]++;
6        }
7        if (attr.CLASS === "PBT") {
8          _stats["PBT"]++;
9        }
10       else if (attr.CLASS === "Non-PBT") {
11         _stats["Non-PBT"]++;
12       }
13       if (attr.METAL === "Yes") {
14         _stats["Metal"]++;
15       }
16     });
17     // Update the values of the ViewModel at once.
18     this.set({
19       count: results.length,
20       stats: _stats
21     });
22   }
```

You can then update the ViewModel with serialized values from the results.

Custom Widget

With your ViewModel in place, you can now create your custom widget.

```
1   // app/widgets/summary.tsx
2   import Widget = require("esri/widgets/Widget");
3
4   import SummaryViewModel, { Stats } from "./viewmodels/
    summaryviewmodel";
5
6   import {
7     aliasOf,
8     subclass,
9     declared,
10    property
11    } from "esri/core/accessorSupport/decorators";
12  import {
13    renderable,
14    join,
15    tsx
16    } from "esri/widgets/support/widget";
17
18  const CSS = {
19    base: "esri-widget esri-component summary-widget",
20    container: "chart-container",
21    column: "summary-column",
22    red: "red",
23    yellow: "yellow",
24    blue: "blue",
25    purple: "purple",
26    keybox: "keybox",
```

```
27      keysection: "keysection"
28    };
29
30    type Style = {
31      target: Stats,
32      multi: number
33    };
34
35    function allValues(x: any) {
36      return Math.max(...(Object.keys(x).map((k) => x[k])));
37    }
38
39    function roundToInt(num: number, target: number) {
40      return Math.round(num / target) * 10;
41    }
42
43    function inlineStyle({ target, multi }: Style) {
44      return Object.keys(target).map(k => {
45        return {
46          height: `${target[k] * multi}px`
47        };
48      });
49    }
50
51    @subclass("app.widgets.summary")
52    class Summary extends declared(Widget) {
53
54      @aliasOf("viewModel.count")
55      @renderable()
56      count: number;
57
```

```
58    @aliasOf("viewModel.stats")
59    @renderable()
60    stats: Stats;
61
62    @property({
63      type: SummaryViewModel
64    })
65    viewModel: SummaryViewModel = new SummaryViewModel();
66
67    render() {
68      const max = roundToInt(allValues(this.stats), 10);
69      const multi = 1;
70      const chartHeight = { height: `${(max * multi)}px` };
71      const styles = inlineStyle({ target: this.stats,
         multi });
72      return (
73        <div class={CSS.base}>
74          <div class={CSS.container}>
75            <label>Facilities Summary ({this.count})</label>
76            <hr />
77            <div id="simpleChart" styles={chartHeight}>
78                <div id="carcinogen" class={join(CSS.column,
                  CSS.red)} styles={styles\
79   [0]}></div>
80                <div id="pbt" class={join(CSS.column, CSS.
                  blue)} styles={styles[1]}>\
81   </div>
82                <div id="non-pbt" class={join(CSS.column,
                  CSS.yellow)} styles={style\
83   s[2]}></div>
```

```
84          <div id="metal" class={join(CSS.column,
            CSS.purple)} styles={styles[\
85  3]]}></div>
86            </div>
87          </div>
88          <section class={CSS.keysection}>
89            <p><div class={join(CSS.keybox, CSS.red)}>
              </div> Carcinogen</p>
90            <p><div class={join(CSS.keybox, CSS.blue)}>
              </div> PBT</p>
91            <p><div class={join(CSS.keybox, CSS.yellow)}>
              </div> Non-PBT</p>
92            <p><div class={join(CSS.keybox, CSS.purple)}>
              </div> Metal</p>
93          </section>
94        </div>
95      );
96    }
97
98  }
99
100 export default Summary;
```

Once you import the dependencies for this module, you create an object that can be used to represent the CSS used for styling your widget.

```
1   ...
2   const CSS = {
3     base: "esri-widget esri-component summary-widget",
4     container: "chart-container",
5     column: "summary-column",
6     red: "red",
```

```
 7      yellow: "yellow",
 8      blue: "blue",
 9      purple: "purple",
10      keybox: "keybox",
11      keysection: "keysection"
12    };
13    ...
```

This is just a nice helper to use during widget development to easily reference CSS styles. You'll see how these are useful when I discuss the render() method.

You will also create a type called Style that you will use in the custom widget.

```
1    ...
2    type Style = {
3      target: Stats,
4      multi: number
5    };
6    ...
```

As you can see, this is going to use the type Stats from your ViewModel. You then provide some helper methods that are used in your widget.

```
1    ...
2    function allValues(x: any) {
3      return Math.max(...(Object.keys(x).map((k) => x[k])));
4    }
5
6    function roundToInt(num: number, target: number) {
7      return Math.round(num / target) * 10;
8    }
9
```

```
10   function inlineStyle({ target, multi }: Style) {
11     return Object.keys(target).map(k => {
12       return {
13         height: `${target[k] * multi}px`
14       };
15     });
16  }
17  ...
```

The first two methods will help you find the maximum values in your chart data so that you can determine the maximum height to your bar charts. The third method is used to create the styles to set the height of each chart bar. You will see how these methods are used in the render() method.

The class for your custom widget has some interesting properties associated with it.

```
1    ...
2    @aliasOf("viewModel.count")
3    @renderable()
4    count: number;
5
6    @aliasOf("viewModel.stats")
7    @renderable()
8    stats: Stats;
9
10   @property({
11     type: SummaryViewModel
12   })
13   viewModel: SummaryViewModel = new SummaryViewModel();
14   ...
```

You have a property count, which is based on viewModel.count, and a property stats, which is based on viewModel.stats. You can use the aliasOf decorator to help define this relationship. You also have to use the renderable decorator for each of these, which lets the widget know that when these values change, you should initialize the render() method again with the new values.

Then you have a property viewModel that you define as having the type SummaryViewModel, which is your custom ViewModel you defined earlier.

Finally, you have your render() method.

```
1    ...
2    render() {
3      const max = roundToInt(allValues(this.stats), 10);
4      const multi = 1;
5      const chartHeight = { height: `${(max * multi)}px` };
6      const styles = inlineStyle({ target: this.stats, multi });
7      return (
8        <div class={CSS.base}>
9          <div class={CSS.container}>
10           <label>Facilities Summary ({this.count})</label>
11           <hr />
12           <div id="simpleChart" styles={chartHeight}>
13             <div id="carcinogen" class={join(CSS.column,
                 CSS.red)} styles={styles\
14   [0]}></div>
15             <div id="pbt" class={join(CSS.column, CSS.
                 blue)} styles={styles[1]}>\
16   </div>
17             <div id="non-pbt" class={join(CSS.column, CSS.
                 yellow)} styles={style\
18   s[2]}></div>
```

```
19              <div id="metal" class={join(CSS.column, CSS.
                purple)} styles={styles[\
20  3]}></div>
21            </div>
22          </div>
23          <section class={CSS.keysection}>
24            <p><div class={join(CSS.keybox, CSS.red)}></div>
              Carcinogen</p>
25            <p><div class={join(CSS.keybox, CSS.blue)}>
              </div> PBT</p>
26            <p><div class={join(CSS.keybox, CSS.yellow)}>
              </div> Non-PBT</p>
27            <p><div class={join(CSS.keybox, CSS.purple)}>
              </div> Metal</p>
28          </section>
29        </div>
30      );
31    }
32  ...
```

The render() method is where the actual widget is defined. As you can see, it looks like you have placed regular HTML into your JavaScript, with some slight differences. You can bind rendered data to properties of the widget. For example, <label>Facilities Summary ({this.count}) </label> will display as <label>Facilities Summary (81)</label> if the count property is 81. When the count property changes, the render method will be called again but will update the DOM with the new value of count.

You first initialize some values to use the helper methods you created.

```
1      ...
2      const max = roundToInt(allValues(this.stats), 10);
3      const multi = 1;
4      const chartHeight = { height: `${(max * multi)}px` };
5      const styles = inlineStyle({ target: this.stats, multi });
6      ...
```

These values will be used to determine the CSS height and color of each category for your chart to display in your custom widget.

I mentioned earlier that you use a CSS object to help you define the CSS for your widget. If you want to combine styles of the CSS object, there is a help method in esri/widgets/support/widget called join.

```
1   <p><div class={join(CSS.keybox, CSS.red)}></div>
Carcinogen</p>
```

This will combine the different CSS classes into a single string when the DOM of the widget is built.

Now you have wired your widget with your ViewModel and the ViewModel with your application store. The ViewModel will handle the business logic of updating the chart data as the map is panned around. The widget will handle the logic to create and display the chart data appropriately. In this case, you have a nice separation of concerns in your application.

You can refer to the completed demo application[19] to see how to implement the custom widget and compile the TypeScript.

---

[19]https://github.com/odoe/esrijs4-ts-demo

Summary

In this chapter, you learned how to use the new widget framework in the ArcGIS API for JavaScript to create a ViewModel and Widget that neatly handle their respective tasks. You now have a pretty good grasp on using some of the helper decorators to simplify the binding of properties to renderable properties. You also have a good understanding of how you can bind property values into JSX for display purposes.

You can find more details about custom widget development in the documentation,[20] in addition to a Hello World sample[21] and a more involved sample.[22] Don't forget that custom widget development does require some familiarity with Accessor.[23] However, the decorators make implementing Accessor much simpler than in regular JavaScript.

---

[20]https://developers.arcgis.com/javascript/latest/guide/custom-widget/index.html

[21]https://developers.arcgis.com/javascript/latest/sample-code/widgets-custom-helloworld/index.html

[22]https://developers.arcgis.com/javascript/latest/sample-code/widgets-custom-recenter/index.html

[23]https://developers.arcgis.com/javascript/latest/guide/implementing-accessor/index.html

Index

A

Accessor.createSubclass(), 63

Accessors

    ArcGIS API for JavaScript, 53

    Object.defineProperty

        method, 53

    property changes, 54–55, 57–58

    watchUtils, 59, 61

addToUI() method, 115

ambientOcclusionEnabled

    property, 87

API core fundamentals

    autocasting, 61–63

    collections, 66–67

    extending accessor, 63–64

    promises, 68

    TypeScript integration, 64–65

ArcGIS API, 15, 110

ArcGIS API 4, 28, 37, 105

ArcGIS Online, 1

ArcGIS Server, 1

Asynchronous Module Definition

    (AMD), 1, 3, 8–10

    geographic information

        systems (GISs), 2

Autocasting, 61–63

B

Beer-related events, 105

C

className property, 107

Collection.prototype.getItemAt()

    method, 66

Content delivery network

    (CDN), 6–7

CSVLayer, 32

D, E

directShadowsEnabled property, 87

displayUTCOffset property, 87

3D scene

    ArcGIS JavaScript API, 73

    camera property, 74–76, 78,

        80–86

    environment property, 87

    local scenes, 88, 90–92, 94–95

    Pictometry Imagery, 71

    Scene Viewer, 72

    WebMap, 72

    WebScene, 72

© Rene Rubalcava 2017

R. Rubalcava, *Introducing ArcGIS API 4 for JavaScript*,

https://doi.org/10.1007/978-1-4842-3282-8

Get the eBook for only $5!

Why limit yourself?

With most of our titles available in both PDF and ePUB format, you can access your content wherever and however you wish—on your PC, phone, tablet, or reader.

Since you've purchased this print book, we are happy to offer you the eBook for just $5.

To learn more, go to http://www.apress.com/companion or contact support@apress.com.

Apress®

Printed in the United States
By Bookmasters